Robert Vashon Rogers

The Law of Hotel Life

The Wrongs and Rights of Host and Guest

Robert Vashon Rogers

The Law of Hotel Life
The Wrongs and Rights of Host and Guest

ISBN/EAN: 9783744667159

Printed in Europe, USA, Canada, Australia, Japan

Cover: Foto ©Suzi / pixelio.de

More available books at **www.hansebooks.com**

THE

LAW OF HOTEL LIFE

OR THE

𝕎rongs and ℝights of ℍost and 𝔾uest.

BY

R. VASHON ROGERS Jr.
Of Osgoode Hall, Barrister-at-Law

SAN FRANCISCO:

SUMNER WHITNEY AND COMPANY.
BOSTON : HOUGHTON, OSGOOD & CO.
The Riverside Press, Cambridge.
1879.

A Preface.

The author knows as well as did old Burton that "books are so plentiful that they serve to put under pies, to lap spice in, and keep roast meat from burning," yet he ventures to offer another volume to the public, trusting that some men's fancies will incline towards and approve of it; for "writings are so many dishes, readers guests, books like beauty— that which one admires another rejects." He thinks he can say, in the words of Democritus Junior, that "as a good housewife out of divers fleeces weaves one piece of cloth, a bee gathers wax and honey out of many flowers, and makes a new bundle of all, I have laboriously collected this cento out of divers authors, and that *sine injuria*. I cite and quote mine authors."

This volume was written at the suggestion of the Publishers, as a companion to "The Wrongs and Rights of a Traveller," and is now committed to the tender mercies of general readers, and to the microscopic eyes of the critics who know everything. Doubtless mistakes will be found; but if every one knew the law who thinks he does, lawyers would starve.

R. V. R. Jr.

Kingston, Ont., March, 1879.

[v]

Contents.

[vii]

CHAPTER I.

A COMMON INN AND INNKEEPER.

The last kiss was given—the last embrace over—
and, amid a storm of hurrahs and laughter and a
hailstorm of old slippers and uncooked rice, we
dashed away from my two-hours' bride's father's
country mansion in the new family carriage, on our
wedding tour. The programme was that we were
to stay at the little village of Blank that night, and
on the morrow we expected to reach the city of
Noname, where we would be able to find convey-
ances more in accord with the requirements of the
last quarter of the nineteenth century of grace
than a carriage and pair.

Arm in arm and hand in hand we sat during the
long, bright June afternoon, as the prancing grays
hurried us along the country roads—now beside
grassy meads, now beneath o'erhanging forest trees,
then up hill, next down dale, while little squirrels
raced along beside us on the fence tops, or little
streamlets dashed along near by, bubbling, foam-
ing, roaring and sparkling in the sheen of the
merry sunshine, and the broad fans of insect an-
gels gently waved over their golden disks as they
floated past; all nature, animate and inanimate,
smiling merrily upon us, as if quite conscious who
and what we were. But little did we note the
beauties of sky or field, cot or hamlet, bird or

flower, for was it not our first drive since the mys-
tic word of the white-robed minister of the Church
had made of us twain one flesh? The beauties of
the other's face and disposition absorbed the con-
templation of each of us. Once or twice, indeed,
I felt inclined to make a remark or two anent the
fields we passed; but remembering that I knew not
a carrot from a parsnip, until it was cooked, or
wheat from oats, except in the well-known forms of
bread and porridge, and not wishing to be like Lord
Erskine, who, on coming to a finely cultivated field
of wheat, called it " a beautiful piece of lavender,"
I refrained.

> Love in itself is very good,
> But 'tis by no means solid food;
> And ere our first day's drive was o'er,
> I found we wanted something more.

So when at last, as the shadows began to lengthen
and still evening drew on, we espied in the valley
beneath us the village in which was our intended
resting place, I exclaimed :
" Ah ! there's our inn at last ! "
" At last ! so soon wearied of my company ! "
chid my bride, in gentle tones. " But why do people talk of a village 'inn' and a city 'hotel'?
What is the difference between a hotel and an
inn ? "
" There is no real difference," I replied, glad to
have the subject changed from the one Mrs. Lawyer had first started. " The distinction is but one
of name, for a hotel is but a common inn on a

grander scale.[1]   Inn, tavern, and hotel are synonymous terms."[2]

"What do the words really mean? "

"Have you forgotten all your French? The
word 'hotel' is derived from the French *hôtel*, (for
hostel,) and originally meant a palace, or residence
for lords and great personages, and has, on that
account no doubt, been retained to distinguish the
more respectable houses of entertainment."

"Well, what is the derivation of 'inn'?" queried my wife.

"I was just going to say that that is rather ob-
scure, but is probably akin to a Chaldaic word
meaning 'to pitch a tent,' and is applicable to all
houses of entertainment.[3] Inns there were in the
far distant East thirty-five centuries and more before you appeared to grace this mundane sphere;[4]
although, when the patriarch Jacob went to visit
his pretty cousins, he was not fortunate enough to
find one, and had to make his bed on the ground,
taking a stone for his pillow."

"And very famous in after years did that just
mentioned pillow become," said Mrs. L., interrupt-
ingly. "And much pain and grief, as well as glory
and renown, has it brought to those who have used
it."

"What meanest thou?" in my turn queried I.

---

[1] Taylor *v.* Monnot, 4 Duer, 116; Jones *v.* Osborn, 2 Chit. 486.
[2] People *v.* Jones, 54 N. Y. (Barb.) 311; St. Louis *v.* Siegrist,
46 Mo. 593.
[3] Wharton's Law of Innkeepers, 8.
[4] Gen. xlii : 27.

" Don't you know that upon that stone the sovereigns of England have been crowned ever since the first Edward stole it from the Scots, who had taken it from the Irish, who doubtless had come honestly by it, and that it now forms one of the wonders and glories of Westminster Abbey ? "

"Indeed!" I remarked, with an inflection in my voice signifying doubt.

" I wonder who kept the first hotel, and what it was like," quoth my lady.

" History is silent on both points," I replied. " But doubtless the early ones were little more than sheds beside a spring or well, where the temporary lodger, worn and dirty, could draw forth his ham sandwich from an antediluvian carpet-bag, eat it at his leisure, wash it down with pure water, curl himself up in a corner, and, undisturbed by the thought of having to rise before daylight to catch the express, sleep—while the other denizens of the cabin took their evening meal at his expense."

" But no one could make much out of such a place," urged Mrs. Lawyer.

" Quite correct. Boniface, in those days, contented himself with an iron coin, a piece of leather stamped with the image of a cow, or some such primitive representative of the circulating medium."

" Times are changed since then," remarked my companion.

" What else could you expect ? Are you a total disbeliever in the Darwinian theory of development ? Inns and hotels, in their history, are excellent examples of the truth of that hypothesis. Protoplasm maturing into perfect humanity is as nothing to them. See how, through many gradations, the primeval well has become the well-stocked bar-room of to-day; the antique hovel is now the luxurious Windsor, the resplendent Palace, the Grand Hôtel du Louvre; the uncouth barbarian, who showed to each comer his own proper corner to lie in, has blossomed into the smiling and gentlemanly proprietor or clerk, who greets you as a man and a brother; the simple charge of a piece of iron or brass for bed and board (then synonymous) has grown into an elaborate bill, which requires ducats, or sovereigns, or eagles to liquidate. But further discussion on this interesting question must be deferred to some future day, for here we are," I added, as we halted at "The Farmer's Home."

"I don't believe that Joseph's brethren ever stopped at a more miserable looking caravansary," said my wife, in tones in which contentment was not greatly marked. "Are you quite sure that this is the inn? It has no sign."

"That fact is of no moment," I hastened to reply. "A sign is not an essential, although it is evidence of an inn. Every one who makes it his business to entertain travelers, and provide lodgings and necessaries for them, their attendants, and horses, is a common innkeeper, whether a sign swings before the door, or no." [1]

"And a common enough innkeeper he looks, in all

[1] Bac. Abr. Iunk. B; Parker v. Flint, 12 Mod. 255; Dickinson v. Rodgers, 4 Humph. (Tenn.) 179.

conscience," said Mrs. Lawyer, as mine host of the signless inn appeared upon the stoop to receive his guests. Coatless he was, waistcoat he had none; the rim of his hat glistened brightly in the declining sun, as if generations of snails had made it their favorite promenade; his legs, or the legs of his pantaloons, were not pairs—they differed so much in length; his boots knew not the glories of Day & Martin; his face had hydrophobia, so long was it since it had touched water; and "wildly tossed from cheek to chin the tumbling cataract of his beard."

With the grace of a bear and the ease of a bull in a china-shop, he ushered us into the parlor, with its yellow floor, its central square of rag-carpet, its rickety table, its antique sampler and gorgeous pictures on the walls, its festoons of colored paper depending from the ceiling, its flies buzzing on the window-panes. Sad were the glances we exchanged when for a minute we were left in this elegant boudoir.

" What a nuisance that the other inn was burnt down last week, and that there is none but this miserable apology for one within thirty miles," I growled.

" 'Tis but for a night," returned my wife, in consolatory tones. " It is only what we might have expected, for saith not the poet:

> ' Inns are nasty, dusty, fusty,
> Both with smoke and rubbish musty' ? "

Soon we mounted the groaning stairs to our

dormitory, and found the house to be a veritable

" Kind of old Hobgoblin Hall,
Now somewhat fallen to decay,
With weather stains upon the wall,
And stairways worn, and crazy doors,
And creaking and uneven floors,
And bedrooms dirty, bare, and small."

The room assigned to us might have been smaller, the furniture might have been cheaper and older— possibly; but to have conceived my blooming bride in a more unsuitable place—impossible. I asked for better accommodation; Boniface shook his head solemnly, (I thought I heard his few brains rattle in his great stupid skull) and muttered that it was the best he had, and if we did not like it we might leave and look elsewhere.

"We must make the best of it, my dear. The landlord is only bound to provide reasonable and proper accommodation, even if there were better in the house; he need not give his guests the precise rooms they may select."[1]

We resolved to display the Christian grace of resignation.

As speedily as possible we arranged our toilets and descended once more to the lower regions, with the faint hope that the dining-room might be better furnished with the good things of this life than either the parlor or bed-room. Sad to relate, the fates were still against us: we found, on enter-

[1] Fell v. Knight, 8 Mees. & W. 269; Doyle v. Walker, 26 Q. B. (Ont.) 502.

ing the *salle à manger*, a couple of small tables put together in the middle of the room, covered with three or four cloths of different ages and dates of washing, and arranged as much like one as the circumstances of the case would allow. Upon these were laid knives and forks; some of the knife-handles were green, others red, and a few yellow, and as all the forks were black, the combination of colors was exceedingly striking. Soon the rest of the paraphernalia and the comestibles appeared, and then Josh Billings' description became strictly applicable; " Tea tew kold tew melt butter ; fride potatoze which resembled the chips a tew-inch augur makes in its journey thru an oke log ; bread solid ; biefstake about az thick as blister plaster, and az tough as a hound's ear ; table kovered with plates ; a few scared-tew-death pickles on one of them, and 6 fly-indorsed crackers on another ; a pewterunktoon kaster, with 3 bottles in it—one without any mustard, and one with tew inches of drowned flies and vinegar in it."

Fortunately, long abstinence came to our aid, and hunger, which covers a multitude of sins in cookery and " dishing up," was present, and our manducatory powers were good ; so we managed to supply the cravings of the inner man to some extent.

" What is this ? " I asked of the landlord, as he handed me a most suspicious looking fluid.

" It's bean soup," he gruffly replied.

" Never mind what it's been—what is it now ? " I asked a second time. A smile from my wife revealed to me my error, and I saved the astonished man the necessity of a reply.

At the table we were joined by an acquaintance, who informed me that he had great difficulty in obtaining admission to the house, as the innkeeper had a grudge against him.

" No matter what personal objection a host may have, he cannot refuse to receive a guest. Every one who opens an inn by the wayside, and professes to exercise the business and employment of a common innkeeper, is bound to afford such shelter and accommodation as he possesses to all travelers who apply therefor, and tender, or are able to pay, the customary charges," [1] I remarked.

" But surely one is not bound to take the trouble to make an actual tender ? " questioned my friend.

" I am not quite so sure on that point," I replied. " Coleridge, J., once said that it is the custom so universal with innkeepers to trust that a person will pay before he leaves the inn, that it cannot be necessary for a guest to tender money before he enters.[2] But, in a subsequent case, Lord Abinger said that he could not agree with Coleridge's opinion,[3] and three other judges concurred with Abinger, although the court was not called upon to decide the matter. In fact, the point has never been definitely settled in England. Text-writers, however,

---

[1] Taylor v. Humphreys, 30 Law J. 262; Watson v. Cross, 2 Duval, (Ky.) 147; Newton v. Trigg, 1 Show. 276; Commonwealth v. Mitchell, 1 Phil. (Pa.) 63.

[2] Rex v. Ivens, 7 Car. & P. 213.

[3] Fell v. Knight, 8 Mees. & W. 276.

think an offer to pay requisite,[1] and it has been so held in Canada."[2]

"But what," said my friend, "if the proprietor is rude enough to slam the door in your face, and you cannot see even an open window?"

"Oh, in that case even Abinger would dispense with a tender."[3]

"It seems hard that a man must admit every one into his house, whether he wishes or no," said my wife.

"Reflect, my dear," I replied, "that if an innkeeper was allowed to choose his guests and receive only those whom he saw fit, unfortunate travelers, although able and willing to pay for entertainment, might be compelled, through the mere caprice of the innkeeper, to wander about without shelter, exposed to the heats of summer, the rains of autumn, the snows of winter, or the winds of spring."

"Do you mean to say that improper persons must be received?"

"Oh dear no! A traveler who behaves in a disorderly or improper manner may be refused admission,[4] and so may one who has a contagious disease, or is drunk.[5] And, of course, if there is no room, admission may be refused.[6] But it will not do for

1 Wharton, p. 78.
2 Doyle v. Walker, 26 Q. B. (Ont.) 502.
3 Fell v. Knight, *supra*.
4 Howell v. Jackson, 6 Car. & P. 742; Moriarty v. Brooks, Ibid. 634.
5 Markham v. Brown, 8 N. H. 523; Fell v. Knight, *supra*.
6 Rex v. Ivens, *supra;* Fell v. Knight, *supra*.

the publican to say that he has no room, if such statement be false; for that venerable authority, Rolle, says: 'Si un hôtelier refuse un guest sur pretense que son maison est pleine de guests, si est soit faux, action sur le case git.' "[1]

"You don't say so!" said my friend, aghast at the jargon. I continued:

"And a publican must not knowingly allow thieves, or reputed thieves, to meet in his house, however lawful or laudable their object may be."[2]

"Suppose they wanted to hold a prayer-meeting, what then?" asked my wife.

"I cannot say how that would be; but a friendly meeting for collection of funds was objected to. Nor should he allow a policeman, while on duty, to remain on his premises, except in the execution of that duty.[3] And he may prohibit the entry of one whose misconduct or filthy condition would subject his guests to annoyance.[4] And I remember reading that Mrs. Woodhull and Miss Claflin were turned away from a New York hotel on the ground of their want of character."

"What if the poor hotel-keeper is sick?" inquired Mrs. Lawyer.

"Neither illness, nor insanity, nor lunacy, nor idiocy, nor hypochondriacism, nor hypochondriasis, nor vapors, nor absence, nor intended absence, can

[1] Roll. Abr. 3 F; White's Case, Dyer, 158.
[2] Marshall v. Fox, Law Rep. 6 Q. B. 370; Markham v. Brown, 8 N.H. 523.
[3] Mullins v. Collins, 43 Law J. M. C. 67.
[4] Markham v. Brown, supra; Pinkerton v. Woodward, 33 Cal. 557.

avail the landlord as an excuse for refusing admission.[1] Although the illness or desertion of his servants, if he has not been able to replace them, might be an excuse; and perchance his own infancy, and perchance not."[2]

"What can you do if he refuses to let you in?" asked my friend. "Break open the door?"

"No, that might lead to a breach of the peace. You may either sue him for damages, or have him indicted and fined; and it is also said in England that the constable of the town, if his assistance is invoked, may force the recalcitrant publican to receive and entertain the guest.[3] If you sue him you will have to prove that he kept a common inn;[4] that you are a traveler,[5] and came to the inn and demanded to be received and lodged as a guest; that he had sufficient accommodation,[6] and refused to take you in, although you were in a fit and proper state to be received,[7] and offered to pay a reasonable sum for accommodation."

"In most hotels they keep a register in which one is expected to inscribe his cognomen by means of a pen of the most villainous description; must one give his name, or may he travel *incog.* and without exhibiting his cacography?"

[1] Bac. Abr. Inns, c. 4; Cross *v.* Andrews, Cro. Eliz. 622.
[2] Addison on Torts, 938. But see Com. Dig. vol. 1, p. 413.
[3] Curw. Hawk. 714.
[4] Cayle's Case, 8 Coke, 32.
[5] Rex *v.* Luellin, 12 Mod. 445; Reg. *v.* Rymner, L. R. 2 Q. B. D. 136.
[6] Fell *v.* Knight, 8 Mees. & W. 269.
[7] Fell *v.* Knight, *supra.*

"An innkeeper has no right to pry into a guest's affairs, and insist upon knowing his name and address,"[1] I replied.

"Talking about registers," began my friend Jones, but in tones so low that what he said must go in the foot notes.[2]

"Last summer," continued talkative Jones, "I tried to get quarters late one Saturday night at a village inn, but the proprietor refused to admit me; and a venerable female put her head out of the window, like Sisera's mother, and told me that they were all in bed, and that they could not take in those who profaned the Sabbath day."

"You might have sued for damages," I said, "for the innkeeper being cosily settled in his bed for the night, or it being Sunday, makes no difference in a traveler's rights;[3] at least where, as in England, it is not illegal to travel on that sacred day."

"I think you said that one must be a traveler before one could claim the rights of a guest—is that an essential?"

"Yes, a *sine qua non*. Bacon says: 'Inns are for

---

[1] Rex *v.* Ivens, 7 Car. & P. 213.

[2] "Did you see that absurd paragraph concerning a traveler who was writing his name in the book when a B. B. sallied out of a crack and took his way slowly and sedately across the page. The newly arrived paused and remarked: 'I've been bled by St. Joe fleas, bitten by Kansas City spiders, and interviewed by Fort Scot graybacks, but I'll be hanged if I ever was in a place before where the bedbugs looked over the hotel register to find out where your room was.'"

"It is generally not necessary for them to take that trouble," I replied.

[3] Rex *v.* Ivens, 7 Car. & P. 213.

2.

passengers and wayfaring men, so that a friend or
a neighbor shall have no action as a guest'[1] (unless,
indeed, the neighbor be on his travels[2]). The Latin
word for an inn is, as of course you know, *diversor-
ium*, because he who lodges there is *quasi divertens
se a via.*"[3]

"What wretched food!" said my wife, as she
helped herself to a biscuit. "'Tis enough to poison
one."

"It is by no means a feast of delicacies—the brains
of singing birds, the roe of mullets, or the sunny
halves of peaches," returned our friend.

"Well, my dear," I replied, "a publican selling
unwholesome drink or victuals may be indicted for
a misdemeanor at common law; and the unhappy
recipient of his noxious mixtures may maintain an
action for the injury done;[4] and this is so even if
a servant provides the goods without the master's
express directions."[5]

    *   *   *   *   *   *

A stroll through the village, and a little moraliz-
ing beside the scarcely cold embers of the rival inn.
where

> " Imagination fondly stooped to trace
> The parlor splendors of that festive place,
> The whitewashed wall, the nicely sanded floor,
> The varnish'd clock that clicked behind the door,"

passed the time until Darkness spread her sable

---

[1] Bac. Abr. vol. 4, p. 448.   [3] Cayle's Case.
[2] Walling *v.* Potter, 35 Conn. 183.   [4] Roll. Abr. 95.
[5] 1 Blackst. Com. 430.

robe over all the earth. We sat outside our inn in the fresh air, and listened while the myriad creatures which seem born on every summer night uplifted in joy their stridulous voices, piping the whole chromatic scale with infinite self-satisfaction. Innumerable crickets sent forth what, perhaps, were gratulations on our arrival; a colony of tree-toads asked, in the key of C sharp major, after their relatives in the back country; while the swell bass of the bull-frogs seemed to be, with deep and hearty utterances, thanking heaven that their dwelling-places were beside pastures green in cooling streams. For a while we listened to this concert of liliputians rising higher and higher as Nature hushed to sleep her children of a larger growth. Ere long, the village bell tolled the hour for retiring. I told the landlady to call us betimes, and then my wife and self shut ourselves up in our little room for the night.

Very weariness induced the partner of my joys and sorrows to commit her tender frame to the coarse bedclothes; but before "tired Nature's sweet restorer, balmy sleep" arrived, and with repose our eyelids closed, an entomological hunt began. First a host of little black bandits found us out, and attacked us right vigorously, skirmishing bravely and as systematically as if they had been trained in the schools of that educator of fleas, Signor Bertolotto, only his students always crawl carefully along and rever hop, as we found by experience that our fierce assailants did. After we had disposed of these light cavalry—these F sharps—for a time, and were again endeavoring to compose our minds to sleep, there

came a detachment of the B-flat brigade, of alder-
manic proportions, pressing slowly on. Again there
was a search as for hidden treasures. Faugh! what
a time we had, pursuing and capturing, crushing
and decapitating, hosts of creatures not to be named
in ears polite. Most hideous night, thou wert not
sent for slumber! It would almost have been better
for us had we been inmates of the hospital for such
creatures at Surat, for there we would have been
paid for the feast we furnished. Here we had the
prospect of paying for our pains and pangs.

I am an ardent entomologist; but I solemnly
avow I grew tired that night of my favorite science.
'Twas vain to think of slumber—

> Not poppy, nor mandragora,
> Nor all the drowsy syrups of the world,

nor yet the plan adopted by the Samoan islanders,
who place a snake, imprisoned in bamboo, beneath
their heads and find the hissing of the reptile highly
soporific, could medicine us to that sweet sleep
which nature so much needed. At length we arose
in despair, donned our apparel, and sat down beside the window to watch for the first bright tints
heralding the advent of the glorious king of day.

"Must we pay for such wretched accommodation?" asked my wife, mournfully. I shook my
head as I replied :

"I fear me so.[1] We might escape;[2] but I don't
want to have a row about my bill in a dollar house."

1 Hart v. Windsor, 12 Mees. & W. 68.
2 Sutton v. Temple, Ibid. 52, 60.

As soon as morning broke we began our preparations for an early departure from the purgatory in
which we had passed the night. When we had
descended, and had summoned the lady of the
house to settle with her, my wife spoke strongly
about the other occupants of our bed.

The woman hotly exclaimed, " You are mistaken,
marm ; I am sure there is not a single flea in the
whole house ! "

"A *single* flea ! " retorted my wife, with wither-
ing scorn ; " a *single* flea ! I should think not ; for
I am sure that they are all married, and have large
families, too."

" Yes," I added,

> 'The little fleas have lesser fleas
> Upon their backs to bite 'em ;
> The lesser fleas have other fleas,
> And so *ad infinitum.* "

CHAPTER II.

CITY HOUSE AND MANNERS.

The next evening, as Mrs. Lawyer and this pres-ent writer were rattling along at the rate of thirty or forty miles an hour in the tail of the iron horse, my bride, imagining that she would like to know somewhat of the law, which had been my mistress for many years, and the *ennui* of the honeymoon having already commenced, asked me what was the legal definition of an inn.

I replied: "The definitions of an inn, like those of lovely woman, are very numerous: but perhaps the most concise is that given by old Petersdorff, who says it is 'a house for the reception and enter-tainment of all comers for gain.'[1] Judge Bayley defined it to be a house where the traveler is fur-nished with everything he has occasion for while on the way."[2]

"I should dearly love to stop at such an inn," broke in my wife. "The worthy host would find my wants neither few nor small."

"Oh, of course, the *everything* is to be taken not only *cum grano salis* but with a whole cellar full of that condiment. For instance, the landlord is not bound to provide clothes or wearing apparel for

---

[1] Peters. Abr. vol. 5, p. 159; Jeremy on Bailments, 139.
[2] Thompson *v.* Lacy, 3 B. & Ald. 203. See also Dickenson *v.* Rodgers, 4 Humph. 179.

his guest.[1] But to proceed with our subject. Best, J., tried his hand—a good one, too—at definition-making, and declared an inn or hotel to be a house, the owner of which holds out that he will receive all travelers and sojourners who are willing to pay a price adequate to the sort of accommodation provided, and who come in a state in which they are fit to be received.[2] Another judge says it is a public house of entertainment for all who choose to visit it as guests without any previous agreement as to the time of their stay or the terms of payment.[3] The judges have, also, got off definitions of the word 'innkeeper.' It has been said that every one who makes it his business to entertain travelers and passengers and provide lodging and necessaries for them and their horses and attendants, is a common innkeeper.[4] But Bacon, very wisely and prudently, adds to this description the important words 'for a reasonable compensation.'[5] One who entertains travelers for payment only occasionally, or takes in persons under an express contract, and shuts his doors upon those whom he chooses, is not an innkeeper, nor is he liable as such.[6] Stables are not necessary to constitute an

[1] Bacon's Abr. Inns, C.

[2] Thompson v. Lacy, 3 B. & Ald. 283.

[3] Wintermute v. Clarke, 5 Sand. 247; Pinkerton v. Woodward, 33 Cal. 557.

[4] Parker v. Flint, 12 Mod. 255; Parkhurst v. Foster, Salk. 287.

[5] Bacon's Abr. Inn. C.

[6] Lyon v. Smith, 1 Morris, 184; State v. Mathews, 2 Dev. & B. 424; Bonner v. Welborn, 7 Geo. 296. But see Commonwealth v. Wetherbee, 101 Mass. 214.

inn;[1] nor is it essential that the meals should be served at *table d'hôte*.[2] A house for the reception and entertainment principally of emigrants arriving at a seaport and usually remaining but a short time, is yet an inn."[3]

Here I stopped because I had nothing more to say; but seeing that my wife was gazing out of the window in a most inattentive manner, yet not wishing her to think that my fund of knowledge was exhausted, I added: "But a truce to this style of conversation. Remember that we are a newly married couple, and are not expected to talk so rationally."

A pause ensued, during which, with great amusement and no little surprise at the facts and doctrines enunciated, we listened to the following dialogue between two rosy-cheeked Englishmen sitting in the seat behind us:

First Briton (*loquitur*).—"How disgusting it is to see those vile spittoons in hotels, in private houses, in churches—everywhere; and notwithstanding that their name is legion, the essence of nicotine is to be seen on all sides, dyeing the floors, the walls, the furniture."

Second Briton.—"I have sometimes doubted whether the Americans expectorate to obtain good luck, or whether it is that they have such good fortune ever attending upon their designs and plans because they expectorate so much."

[1] Thompson v. Lacy, *supra*.
[2] Krohn v. Sweeny, 2 Daly, N. Y. 200.
[3] Willard v. Reinhardt, 2 E. D. Smith, 148.

First B. (rather dazed).—"I don't understand you."

Second B. (in tones of surprise at the other's want of comprehension).—"Don't you know that many Englishmen spit if they meet a white horse, or a squinting man, or a magpie, or if, inadvertently, they step under a ladder, or wash their hands in the same basin as a friend? In Lancashire, boys spit over their fingers before beginning to fight, and travelers do the same on a stone when leaving home, and then throw it away, and market people do it on the first money they receive."

First B. (interrogatively).—"But, if these dirty people do indulge in this unseemly habit, what then?"

Second B.—"Why, they consider it a charm that will bring good luck, or avert evil. Swedish peasants expectorate thrice if they cross water after dark. The old Athenians used to spit if they passed a madman. The savage New Zealand priest wets two sticks with his saliva when he strives to divine the result of a coming battle."

First B.—"But the why and the wherefore of all this expectoration?"

Second B.—"Because the mouth was once considered the only portal by which evil spirits could enter into a man, and by which alone they could be forced to make their exit; and the idea was to drive the fiends out with the saliva. The Mussulmans made spitting and nose-blowing a part of their religious ceremonies, for they hoped thereby to free themselves from the demons which they believed filled the air; and a Kamtschatkan priest, after he has sprinkled with holy water the babe brought to the baptismal font, spits solemnly to north and south, to east and west."

A wild shriek of the locomotive, announcing that we were drawing near our destination, and the necessary preparations consequent upon such arrival, prevented us listening further to this conversation. I remarked to my wife that if I had never known of evil spirits being laid by the efflux of saliva, I had at least heard of their being raised thereby, and instanced Shylock and Signor Antonio.

We drove up to the "Occidental House" in the bus belonging to that famous establishment. The satchel of a fellow-traveler was lost off the top of the carriage. I endeavored to console him with the information that years ago, where the keeper of a public house gave notice that he would furnish a free conveyance to and from the cars to all passengers, with their baggage, and for that purpose employed the owner of certain carriages to take passengers and their baggage, free of charge, to his house, and a traveler, who knew of this arrangement, drove in one of these cabs to the hotel, and on the way there had his trunk lost or stolen through the want of skill or care of the driver, the innkeeper was held liable to make good the loss. The court that decided the point held that it was immaterial whether he was responsible as a common carrier or as an innkeeper, as in either case the consideration for the undertaking was the profit to be derived from the entertainment of the traveler as a guest, and that an implied promise to take care of the baggage was founded on such consideration.[1]

My fellow-traveler seemed not a little pleased with my information, and expressed his intention of seeking an early interview with the landlord of the "Occidental" on the subject of the lost satchel.

While in the bus, a man who appeared to be an agent for a rival house made some very disparaging remarks with regard to the "Occidental," with more vehemence than elegance or truthfulness, evidently with the design of inducing some intending guests to change their minds and go elsewhere. It was well for him that none of the "Occidental" people heard him, for if they had he might speedily have become the defendant in an action at law, for misstatements like his are actionable.[2]

What a contrast between the palatial mansion at which we now alighted, and the hovel which the previous night had covered our heads—(protection it had not afforded). The small and dirty entrance of the one was exchanged for a spacious and lofty hall in the other, paved with marble and fitted up with comfortable sofas and cushions, on which was lounging and smoking, talking and reading, a multifarious lot of humanity; the parlor, with its yellow paint and rag carpet, was replaced by large, well lighted and elegantly furnished drawing-rooms, with carpets so soft that a footstep was no more heard than a passing shadow, and gorgeous mirrors reflecting the smiles, faces and elaborately artistic

---

[1] Dickinson v. Winchester, 4 Cush. 114.
[2] Bacon's Abr. Inns, B.

toilets of city belles, and the trim figures and prim
moustaches of youthful swells; a pretty little room,
yclept an elevator, neatly carpeted, well lighted,
free from noxious scents, with comfortable seats
and handsome reflectors, led up on high, instead of
the groaning, creaking stairs of the country inn.
The bedrooms, with their spotless linen, luxurious
beds, dainty carpets, and cosy chairs, rested and
refreshed one's weary bones by their very appearance. The noble dining-hall, with its delicately
tinted walls, its pillars and gilded roof, with neatly
dressed waiters, and the master of ceremonies pa-
trolling the room seeing to the comfort of the guests,
the arrangements of their places, and that each
servant did his duty, gave a zest to one's appetite
which the tempting viands increased a hundred fold,
and the soups, fish, relèves, entrées, game, relishes,
vegetables, pastry, and dessert of the *menu* differed
from the bill of fare of the previous day as does
light from darkness, sweet from bitter.

As we were ascending in the luxuriously furnished,
brilliantly lighted and gently moving elevator, a nin-
nyhammer tried to get on after the conductor had
started. In doing so he well nigh severed the con-
nection between his ill-stored head and well-fed
body. I told him that his conduct was most fool-
hardy, for if he had been injured he could have
recovered nothing from the hotel proprietor, for
the accident would have been directly traceable to
his own stupid want of ordinary care and prudence.[1]

[1] Robinson *v.* Cove, 22 Vt. 213; Butterfield *v.* Forrester, 11
East, 60; Rathbun *v.* Payne, 19 Wend. 399.

At the dinner table we found that many of the people, notwithstanding the luxurious surroundings, seemed quite oblivious of the sage advice given by Mistress Hannah Woolley, of London, in the year of grace 1673. That worthy says in her "Gentlewoman's Companion": "Do not eat spoon-meat so hot that tears stand in your eyes, or that thereby you betray your intolerable greediness. Do not bite your bread, but cut or break it; and keep not your knife always in your hand, for that is as unseemly as a gentlewoman who pretended to have as little a stomach as she had mouth, and therefore would not swallow her peas by spoonfuls, but took them one by one and cut them in two before she would eat them. Fill not your mouth so full that your cheeks shall swell like a pair of Scotch bag-pipes."

One of the company near by ate as if he had never eaten in any place save a shanty all the days of his life; he was not quite so bad, however, as the celebrated Dr. Johnson, who, Lord Macaulay tells us, "tore his dinner like a famished wolf, with the veins swelling in his forehead, and the perspiration running down his cheeks;" but yet, in dispatching his food, he swallowed two-thirds of his knife at every mouthful with the coolness of a juggler.

"Such a savage as that ought not to be permitted to take his meals in the dining-room," said my wife.

"I am not sure that he could be prevented on account of his style of eating," I replied, as the man began shoveling peas with a knife into his mouth, which could not have been broader unless Dame Nature had placed his auricular appendages an inch

8.

or two further back. (By the way, how did they
eat peas before the days of knives, forks, and
spoons?)

"Do you mean to say that if an individual makes
himself so extremely disagreeable to all other guests,
the proprietor has no right to ask him to leave?"
queried Mrs. L.

"Well, my dear, it was held in Pennsylvania that
the host might request such an one to depart; and
that if he did not, the hotel-keeper might lay his
hands gently upon him and lead him out, and if resistance was made might use sufficient force to ac-
complish the desired end."[1]

"Then please tell that waiter to take that man
out," broke in my wife.

"Not so fast, my dear; that decision was reversed
afterward, and it was said to be assault and battery
so to eject a guest.[2] I have known $600 damages
given to a guest for an assault on him by his landlord.[3] I remember, too, a case where a man rejoicing
in the trisyllabic name of Prendergast was coming
from Madras to London round the Cape of Storms,
having paid his fare as a cabin passenger. His habit
was to reach across others at table to help himself,
and to take potatoes and broiled bones in his fingers,
devouring them as was the fashion in the days when
Adam delved and Eve span, if they had such things
then. The captain, offended at this ungentlemanly
conduct, refused to treat Master P. as a first-class

---

[1] Commonwealth v. Mitchell, 2 Pars. Sel. Cas. 431.
[2] Commonwealth v. Mitchell, 1 Phila. 63.
[3] Kelsey v. Henry, 49 Ill. 488.

passenger, excluded him from the cabin, and would not allow him to walk on the weather side of the ship. On reaching England, Prendergast sued the captain for the breach of his agreement to carry him as a cuddy passenger; the officer pleaded that the conduct of the man had been vulgar, offensive, indecorous and unbecoming, but the son of Neptune was mulcted in damages to the tune of £25, Chief Justice Tindal observing that it would be difficult to say what degree of want of polish would, in point of law, warrant a captain in excluding one from the cuddy. Conduct unbecoming a gentleman in the strict sense of the word might possibly justify him, but in this case there was no imputation of the want of gentlemanly principles.[1] But here, at last, comes our dinner; let us show our neighbors how to handle knife and fork aright."

And a very good dinner it was, too, although dished by a cook who had not the talents of the ancient knights of the kitchen who could dexterously serve up a sucking-pig boiled on one side and roasted on the other, or make so true a fish out of turnips as to deceive sight, taste, and smell. These antique masters of the gastronomic art knew how to suit each dish to the need and necessity of each guest. They held to the doctrine that the more the nourishment of the body is subtilized and alembicated, the more will the qualities of the mind be rarefied and quintessenced, too. For a young man destined to live in the atmosphere of a royal court, whipped cream and calves' trotters were supplied

[1] Prendergast v. Compton, 8 Car. & P. 454.

by them; for a sprig of fashion, linnets' heads,
essence of May beetles, butterfly broth, and other
light trifles; for a lawyer destined to the chicanery
of his profession and for the glories of the bar,
sauces of mustard and vinegar and other condiments of a bitter and pungent nature would be
carefully provided.[1] As Lord Guloseton says, "The
ancients seem to have been more mental, more
imaginative, than we in their dishes; they fed their
bodies, as well as their minds, upon delusion : for
instance, they esteemed beyond all price the tongues
of nightingales, because they tasted the very music
of the birds in the organ of their utterance. That
is the poetry of gastronomy."

I noticed at a table near by a merry party. I
afterward learned that it was composed of a number of fast young men from the city, who had come
in to have a good dinner, and exhibit themselves,
their garments, and their graces before the assembled guests; and that, when the hour of reckoning
came, the needful wherewith to liquidate the little
bill was not forthcoming. The landlord insisted
that each one was liable for the whole, as there was
no special agreement, (and this would generally be
the case[2]) and that one who was solvent should pay
the reckoning for all; but, unfortunately for Boniface, his clerk had been told beforehand that that
moneyed man was the guest of the others, who
were all as poor as Job's peahens; so that the poor
man had no recourse against the deadheads, in this

[1] Dons de Comus, Paris, 1758.
[2] Foster v. Taylor, 3 Camp. N. P. 49.

direction, at all events,[1] and even the moneyed gent got a free dinner. The worthies swaggered out, singing in an undertone the words of an Ethiopian minstrel appropriate to the occasion.

* * * * *

As my wife was returning to her room after dinner, she met a poor woman, whose daily walk in life was from the wash-tub to the clothes-line, looking in vain for some miserable sinner who had departed leaving his laundry bill unpaid. After endeavoring in vain to console the woman, Mrs. Lawyer, (who had a Quixotic way of interfering in other people's troubles) came running back to me to ask if the hotel-keeper was not bound to pay for the washing. I told her of course not, unless he had been in the habit of paying the laundry bills of guests who had left; then an undertaking to that effect might be inferred, and it might be considered as evidence of an antecedent promise.[2] With this small crumb of comfort, my wife returned to the user of soap and destroyer of buttons.

While sitting, *a la* Mr. Briggs, in the smoking-room, "with my waistcoat unbuttoned, to give that just and rational liberty to the subordinate parts of the human commonwealth which the increase of their consequence after the hour of dinner naturally demands," and gently, (as good Bishop Hall puts it) "whiffing myself away in nicotian incense to the idol of my intemperance," a fellow-puffer spoke to me about the excessive charges of the house.

[1] Foster *v.* Taylor, 3 Camp. N. P. 49.
[2] Collard *v.* White, 1 Starkie, 171.

I told him that in the good old days of yore, and perchance even yet, an innkeeper who charged exorbitant prices might be indicted, and that our ancestors were wont to have the rates fixed by public proclamation.[1]

He then remarked that he would not mind about the prices, if the landlord had allowed him to do a little business in the place.

"Your right to lodge and be fed in the house gives you no right to carry on trade here,"[2] I replied.

"One of the waiters threatened to kick me yesterday for doing business."

"Oh, if you are assaulted by any of the servants, the proprietor is liable to you in damages, though he was not himself present at the time, or even consenting thereto,"[3] I returned. Then, fearing lest I might be nourishing a viper in the shape of a book-agent, or vendor of patent articles, I left the room, the words of the poet running through my brain:

> "Society is now one polished horde,
> Formed of two mighty tribes—the Bores and Bored."

[1] Bacon's Abr. Inns, C.
[2] Ambler *v.* Skinner, 7 Rob. (N. Y.) 561.
[3] Wade *v.* Thayer, 40 Cal. 578.

CHAPTER III.

ACCIDENTS, ROOMS, DOGS.

Next morning, as we were arranging whither we would wend our way, I proposed taking a bus. My wife remarked positively that she wished that I would not use that vulgar word. I returned:

"Humph! Did you ever hear the story about Lord Campbell and the omnibus?"

"What was it?" she asked.

"A lawyer while arguing before him continually spoke of a certain kind of carriage as 'a brougham,' (pronouncing both syllables) whereupon his lordship, with that pomposity for which he was rather noted, remarked that 'broom' was the more usual, and not incorrect, pronunciation; that such pronunciation was open to no grave objection, and had the great advantage of saving the time consumed by uttering an extra syllable. Shortly afterward Campbell spoke of an 'omnibus.' The counsel whom he had shortly before corrected, jumped up with such promptitude that the judge was startled into silence, exclaiming: 'Pardon me, my Lord, the carriage to which you draw attention is usually called 'a bus': that pronunciation is open to no grave objection, and has the great advantage of saving the time consumed by uttering *two* extra syllables.' You can easily draw the moral from that little tale, my dear."

[31]

Into a bus we got, and out of it we got, in course of time. We went up and down and in and out and roundabout, seeing the sights and doing the town like many another couple had done before us, and will do again during that most awkward of seasons, the honeymoon.

While my spouse gazed in at some lovely silks, sweet feathers, and ducks of bonnets, unmindful of the troubles that Moses underwent in obtaining the latter part of the Decalogue, I took the opportunity of instilling some legal doctrines and decisions into her head.

"Remember," I said, "the solemn words of the poet:

'Man wants but little here below,
    Nor wants that little long.' "

"I fear that a woman like myself will have to wait very long before she gets her little wants supplied," she saucily interjected.

"I was about to remark," I sternly continued, "that if you are very extravagant in your wardrobe and tastes, I will not be liable to pay all your little bills. Once upon a time an English judge decided that a milliner could not make a husband pay £5,287 for bonnets, laces, feathers and ribbons supplied to his dear little wife during a few months."[1]

"No power on earth could make you pay that sum, or anything like it; so don't worry yourself, my darling," coolly and somewhat sarcastically remarked Mrs. Lawyer.

"Please do not interrupt. In another case it was

[1] Lane v. Ironmonger, 13 Mees. & W. 368.

held that the price of a sea-side suit, some £67, could not be collected from a husband—a poor barrister—who had forbidden his wife to go to the watering place."[1]

"He must have been a very poor lawyer if he never had a suit that cost more to some unfortunate client."

"Again, the Rev. Mr. Butcher "——

"I like that name for a parson," again interposed my wife. "It suggests, you know, a slender frame, a pale face, taper fingers."

I paid no heed, but went on:

——" Was excused payment of some £900 for birds—lorees, avadavats, lovebirds, quakers, cutthroats—furnished his wife during the short space of ten months."[2]

" But I will not be as extravagant as any of those misguided ladies were," remarked my wife, most sensibly.

" Well, then, there will be no trouble. Everything necessary I will of course pay for willingly, as I could be made to pay for them, if unwilling. Even a piano, perhaps, I will stand;[3] or false teeth;[4] but, mind you, not quack medicines,[5] though you are a duck."

" I am glad to hear ' that you'll vouchsafe me raiment, bed, and food '; please begin now with the last named necessary article, for I am hungry." Mrs. Lawyer was a practical woman.

---

[1] Atkins v. Carwood, 7 Car. & P. 759.
[2] Freestone v. Butcher, 9 Car. & P. 643.
[3] Parke v. Kleeber, 37 Pa. St. 251.
[4] Gilman v. Andrus, 28 Vt. 241.
[5] Wood v. Kelly, 8 Cush. 406.

"I presume it is time for lunch," I replied. "Ah me! I wish lawyers in this nineteenth century could get their dinners as cheaply as they could in days gone by, when the client paid therefor, as appears in many an ancient register. The clerk of St. Margaret's, Westminster, entered on his books that he paid to Robert Fylpott, learned in the law, for his counsel given, 3s. 8d., with 6d. for his dinner. *Tempora mutantur*. There's a restaurant. Let us enter."

We entered accordingly, and a very good luncheon we had, except for one slight *contretemps*. While engaged upon my macaroni soup, a long, reddish thread—as I surmised—revealed itself to my vision. Calling the waiter, I demanded how it came there.

"Ah!" said the man, quite cheerfully, "I can tell you where that came from. Our cook's in love, sir, and is constantly opening a locket containing a lock of his sweetheart's hair. Of course, some of it occasionally falls into the dishes."

"Disgusting!" said my wife.

"Beastly!" said I.

The waiter calmly continued: "Beg pardon, sir, but would you mind giving me the hair? You see, the cook is so fond of her that he is quite pleased when I bring him back a stray hair or two."

Of course, I knew that accidents will, &c.; and everything else was very good. My wife, however, wasted a good deal of time in listening in wondering amazement to the calculations made at an adjoining table.

"I don't see how a waiter can remember such a long list of things, and tell what they all come to so rapidly ; or how any two men could eat as much as those two did," she remarked to me.

"Pshaw!" I replied, "that is nothing to Mr. Smallweed's arithmetical powers, or to the gastronomic achievements of himself and his friends."

"And pray what did Mr. S. do?" asked my wife.

"Why, when their little luncheon was over, and he was asked by the pretty waitress what they had had, he replied, without a moment's hesitation: 'Four veals and hams is 3 and 4 potatoes is 3 and 4 and one summer cabbage is 3 and 6 and 3 marrows is 4 and 6 and 6 breads is 5 and 3 Cheshires is 5 and 3 and 4 pints of half-and-half is 6 and 3 and 4 small rums is 8 and 3 and 3 Pollys is 8 and 6 and 8 and 6 in half a sovereign, Polly, and 18 pence out.'"

When we rose to leave the room, we found that some one had left before us with Mrs. Lawyer's new umbrella. Silently I quitted the place, for I knew that it had been decided that a restaurant is not an inn, so as to charge the proprietor with the liabilities of an innkeeper toward transient persons who take their meals there ; (and the same rule applies even though he does in fact keep in the same building an hotel, to which the eating-house is attached;[1]) and therefore it would be useless to expect the proprietor to make good the loss. Nor is a refreshment bar (where persons casually passing by receive the good things of this life at a counter) an inn,

---

[1] Carpenter *v.* Taylor, 1 Hilt. (N. Y.) 193.

although it is connected with an hotel, and kept
under the same license, but entered by a separate
door from the street.[1]   Where, however, a servant
once asked permission to leave a parcel at a tavern,
and the landlady refused to receive it; the man,
being a thirsty soul, called for something to drink,
putting the parcel on the floor behind him while
imbibing, and while thus the spirit was descending
more rapidly than it ever did in the most sensitive
thermometer, the package disappeared, and never
was seen again by the owner; yet the innkeeper
was held responsible for the loss.[2]

An umbrella was bought and money expended
for divers little odds and ends before we went back
to the hotel for dinner.   On our return, Mr. Deadhead and his wife entered the hotel just before us.
They were country cousins of the proprietor's, and
had been asked to dinner, or had come without an
invitation.   As he was opening an inside door a
large pane of glass fell out of it, and, slightly graz-
ing his hand, shivered into a thousand pieces on the
marble floor.   I told him to rejoice that he had been
fortunate enough to escape with the loss of but a
drop or two of his vital fluid; for I remembered
distinctly a similar accident happening to my father's old friend, Southcote, in England, years ago;
and although he sued the proprietor of the house,
alleging that he (the landlord) was possessed of an
hotel, into which he had invited S. as a visitor, and

---

[1] Regina v. Rymer, L. R. 2 Q. B. D. 136.
[2] Bennett v. Mellor, 5 T. R. 276.   See, also, Houser v. Tully,
62 Pa. St. 92.

in which there was a glass door which it was necessary for him (S.) to open for the purpose of leaving, and which he, by the permission of the owner, and with his knowledge, and without any warning from him, lawfully opened, for the purpose aforesaid, as a door which was in a proper condition to be opened, yet, by and through the carelessness, negligence, and default of defendant, the door was then in an insecure and dangerous condition, and unfit to be opened; and, by reason of said door being in such insecure and dangerous condition, and of the then carelessness, negligence, default, and improper conduct of the defendant in that behalf, a large piece of glass fell from the door, and wounded Southcote—yet, although he said all this, the Court of Exchequer, with Pollock, C. B, at its head, decided that no cause of action against the proprietor was disclosed.[1] It was considered that a visitor in a house was in the same position as any other member of the establishment, so far as regards the negligence of the master or his servants, and must take his chance of accidents with the rest.[2] Baron Bramwell, however, well said that where a person is in the house of another, either on business or for any other lawful purpose, he has a right to expect that the owner will take reasonable care to protect him from injury, and will not leave trap-doors open down which he might fall, or take him into a garden among spring-guns and man-traps.[3]

At dinner—to which, in addition to the various

[1] Southcote v. Stanley, 1 Hurl. & N. 247. [2] Per Pollock, B. C. [3] Ibid.

4.

condiments provided by mine host, we ourselves
brought that best of sauces, hunger—there was seated at a neighboring table Mrs. Deadhead, a friend
of the proprietor's, as I have said, a lady of considerable amplitude of person, and extensively be-
decked with the diamonds of Golconda, the gold
of Australia, the lace of Lyons, the feathers of
South Africa, the millinery of New York, and
attired in a silk dress of most fashionable shape,
color, and make. As a waiter was helping this very
conspicuous member of society to a plate of soup,
he caught his foot in the extensive train, stumbled,
and placed the soup in her ladyship's lap—minus
the plate. Great was the commotion, loud the re-
proaches, abject the apologies.

My wife thereupon whispered to me that the
upset would not have mattered much if the soup
was any like hers.

"Why not?" I queried, in some surprise, and
anxious to learn as speedily as possible the chemi-
cal peculiarities of a lady's toilet.

"Because then the dress would have been turned
into a watered silk," was the only answer I got.

It was some time before I saw the point, and
then I smiled a dreary, weary smile, and remarked
that I hoped the lady was able to re-dress herself,
for I thought that she could get no redress from
the proprietor—at least, that legal luminary, Pollock, C. B., so insinuated on one occasion.[1]

My wife grew fidgety because the waiters were
somewhat tardy in filling her orders.

[1] Southcote v. Stanley, *supra.*

"Look," she said, "at those lazy fellows! Half a dozen of them doing nothing, while we are kept waiting, still waiting."

"Doubtless," I replied, "they have been deeply impressed with the truth of that grand old Miltonic line :

'They also serve who only stand to wait.'"

*   *   *   *   *

While taking my post-prandial smoke, my interrogator of the previous evening again approached me, and asked, in a grumbling voice, if the landlord had a right to turn him out of one room, and put him into another.

"Oh, yes," I replied ; "he has the sole right of selecting the apartment for each guest, and, if he finds it expedient, may change the room and assign his patron another. There is no implied contract that one to whom a particular room has been given shall retain it so long as he chooses to pay for it.[1] You pay your money, but you don't take your choice."

"But I liked the room so much," said Mr. Complaining Grumbler.

"It matters not. The proprietor is not bound to comply with your caprices.[2] When you go to an hotel you have only a mere easement of sleeping in one room, and eating and drinking in another, as Judge Maule once remarked."[3]

"Can he turn me out of the house altogether?"

"Certainly not, if you behave yourself; unless,

[1] Doyle v. Walker, 26 Q. B. (Ont.) 502.
[2] Fell v. Knight, 8 Mees. & W. 276.
[3] Lane v. Dixon, 3 M. G. & S. 784.

indeed, you neglect or refuse to pay your bill upon reasonable demand."[1]

"I am going away by the night train," said Mr. C. G., "and I did not wish to go to bed; so he insisted upon taking my room, and told me I might stay in the parlor until I left."

"And quite right, too. Although he cannot make you go to bed, or turn you out of doors because you do not choose to sleep, still you cannot insist upon having a bed-room in which to sit up all night, if you are furnished with another room proper for that purpose."[2]

"I intend returning in the afternoon; can he refuse to take care of my traps while I am absent?"

"I fancy not, for a temporary absence does not affect the rights of a guest.[3] Long since, it was laid down as law that if one comes to an inn with a hamper, in which he has goods, and goes away, leaving it with the host, and in a few days comes back, but in the meantime his goods are stolen, he has no action against the host, for at the time of stealing he was not his guest, and by keeping the hamper the innkeeper had no benefit, and therefore is not chargeable with the loss of it. But it would be otherwise if the man is absent but from morn to dewy eve;[4] and where, in New York State, a guest, after spending a few days at an hotel, gave up his room, left his valise—taking a check for it—

[1] Doyle v. Walker, supra.
[2] Fell v. Knight, 8 Mees. & W. 276.
[3] McDonald v. Edgerton, 5 Barb. (N. Y.) 560.
[4] Bacon's Abr. Inns, C; Gelley v. Clark, Cro. J. 188.

and was gone eight days, without paying his bill; on returning, he registered his name, took a room, and called for his bag, when another appeared in its place, having the duplicate check attached : the Court of Common Pleas held that, whether the case was considered as an ordinary bailment, or as property in an innkeepers' hands, on which he had a lien, he was bound to exercise due care and diligence, and that he must account for the loss, the changing of the check being evidence of negligence." [1]

I rose to leave the room, for I was growing weary of this catechetical performance; but my questioner's budget was not yet exhausted, and, as I made my exit, I heard him say :

" Pardon me—one inquiry more : I was at the St. Nicholas last week when it was burnt down, and I lost some of my clothes. Is the owner liable to make good the damage sustained?" [2]

I heeded not, and went to seek my wife. After some search through the magnificent drawing-rooms of our sumptuous hotel, I at length found her in an elegant parlor, seated at a piano, and gently playing some sweet melodies. As I approached, she motioned me to be cautious. When I reached her, I saw that a large spider was stationed at the edge of the piano cover, apparently drinking in the harmony of sweet sounds to the utmost extent of his arachnidian nature. My advent broke the spell, and away the little hairy darkey rushed,

[1] Murray v. Clarke, 2 Daly, (N. Y.) 102.
[2] For answer, see page 103.

hand over hand, up his tiny cable of four thousand twisted strands, till he was safe in the cornice of the ceiling. My wife was charmed at her novel listener, and exclaimed: " Did you ever see such a thing?"

"No, but I have read of it," I replied. "Michelet, in his charming book on 'The Insect,' tells that a little musical prodigy, who at eight astounded and stupefied his hearers by his mastery of the violin, was forced to practice long weary hours in solitude. There was a spider, however, in the room, which, entranced by the melodious strains, grew more and more familiar, until at length it would climb upon the mobile arm that held the bow. Little Berthome needed no other listener to kindle his enthusiasm. But a cruel step-mother appeared on the scene suddenly one day, and with a single blow of her slipper annihilated the octopedal audience. The child fell to the ground in a deathlike faint, and in three months was a corpse—dead from a broken heart."

"How sad!" said Mrs. Lawyer, in husky tones, as she blew her nose in a suspicious manner.

"Then there was also the musical spider of Pellison"—— A little snarleyow of a dog here rushed in and barked so vigorously and furiously that my wife never heard more of that spider. I tried to turn the wretched creature out, but a puppy following—the owner—requested me to leave it alone. I must say that I heartily concur with Mr. Justice Manisty (and I sincerely trust that my concurrence will afford encouragement to the learned gentleman in his arduous office) in holding that a guest cannot, under any circumstances, insist upon bringing a dog into any room in a hotel where other guests are. On the same occasion on which Judge Manisty expressed his views, Kelly, C. B., remarked that he would not lay down the rule positively that under no circumstances would a guest have a right to bring a dog into an inn; there might possibly, he observed, b; circumstances in which, if a person came to an inn with a dog, and the innkeeper refused to put up the animal in any stable or outbuilding, and there was nothing that could make the canine a cause of alarm or an annoyance to others, its owner might be justified in bringing it into the house. His lordship, however, considered that a landlord had a right to refuse to provide for the wants of a visitor who insisted upon coming with two very large St. Bernard mastiffs, one a fierce creature, that had to be muzzled, the other a dog of a gentler nature, but somewhat given to that bad habit referred to in those Proverbs of Solomon which the men of Hezekiah, king of Judah, copied out, and by the apostle St. Peter in his second epistle.[1]

*   *   *   *   *

The next day there was a gentle ripple of excitement pervading the house. Two cases of larceny came to light, and made the guests communicative and talkative.

In one case a Mr. Blank, his wife, and amiable and accomplished daughter, (I can vouch for the

[1] Regina *v.* Rymer, L. R. 2 Q. B. D. 141.

correctness of these adjectives; for I had a very pleasant chat—to call it by a mild name—with her one day, while Mrs. Lawyer was lying down after dinner) had a sitting-room and bedroom *en suite*, so arranged that when the sitting-room door was open one could see the entrances into both bedrooms. Mrs. B., being in her room, laid upon the bed her reticule, in which was a by no means despicable sum of money. She then rejoined her spouse and daughter in the sitting-room, leaving the door between the two apartments open. Some five minutes after, she sent Miss Blank—who was not too proud to run a short errand for her kind mamma—for the bag; but lo! it was gone, and was never again found by a member of the Blank family; for

"In vain they searched each cranny of the house,
    Each gaping chink impervious to a mouse."

The other robbery was of the goods of a young Englishman, who, the previous evening, had been boastfully exhibiting some sovereigns in the smoking-room. When he went to bed he had placed his watch and money on a table in his room, left his door open, and, on morning dawning, was surprised to find his time-piece and cash vanished with the early dew. Other people would have been surprised if they had remained.

I fell into conversation on the subject of these depredations with a gentleman whom I afterward discovered to be a member of Lincoln's Inn, a place which bears very little resemblance to our American hotels.

" 'Tis very strange," said Mr. Learned Inthelaw, "how history repeats itself, even in insignificant matters."

I bowed, and remarked : "A very sensible man once observed that there was nothing new under the sun."

"He did not live, however, in this our nineteenth century," was the reply. "But what I was going to say was that there are two cases reported in our English law-books exactly similar to the two occurrences of to-day."

"That is singular. What were the decisions?"

"In the reticule case,[1] the hotel-keeper was held responsible for the loss; in the other,[2] it was considered that the guest had been guilty of negligence so as to absolve the host. You know that with us it was decided, about the time that Columbus was discovering America, that an innkeeper is liable for the goods of his guests if damaged or stolen while under his care as an innkeeper;[3] and in such cases he is not freed from his grave responsibility by showing that neither himself nor his servants are to blame, but in every event he is liable unless the loss or injury is caused by the act of God, or the queen's enemies, or the fault, direct or implied, of the guest[4]—and that even though the poor man has not only not been negligent, but has even been diligent in his efforts to save the property of his guest."[5]

[1] Kent v. Shuckard, 2 Barn. & Adol. 803.
[2] Cashill v. Wright, 6 El. & B. 89.
[3] Year Book, 10 Henry VII, 26.
[4] Morgan v. Ravey, 6 Hurl. & N. 265.
[5] Ibid.

"The rule is the same with us,"[1] I replied, "and it extends to all personal property the guest brings with him, whatever may be the value or the kind.[2] And if the proprietor happens to be absent he is still liable for the conduct of those he has left in charge.[3] Innkeepers, as well as common carriers, are regarded as insurers of the property committed to their care. The law rests on the same principles of policy here as in England and other countries, and is wise and reasonable."[4]

"But it seems very severe upon innkeepers," remarked a by-stander.

"Rigorous as the law may seem, my dear sir," replied my friend of Lincoln's Inn, "and hard as it may actually be in one or two particular instances, yet it is founded on the great principle of public utility to which all private considerations ought to yield; for travelers, who must be numerous in a rich and commercial country, are obliged to rely almost implicitly on the good faith of innkeepers, whose education and morals are often none of the best, and who might have frequent opportunities for associating with ruffians and pilferers; while the injured guest could seldom or never obtain legal proof of such combinations, or even of their negligence, if no actual fraud had been committed by them."[5]

"What did the old Roman law say on the sub-

[1] Shaw v. Berry, 31 Me. 478; Sibley v. Aldrich, 33 N. H. 553.

[2] Kellogg v. Sweeney, 1 Lans. (N. Y.) 397.

[3] Rockwell v. Proctor, 39 Ga. 105.

[4] Wilde, J., Mason v. Thompson, 9 Pick. 280.

[5] Jones on Bailments, pp. 95–96.

ject?" inquired old Dr. Dryasdust, who considered
that nothing done or said on the hither side of the
Middle Ages was worthy of consideration.

"They, sir, were equally anxious to protect the
public against dishonest publicans, and by their
edicts gave an action against them if the goods of
travelers were lost or hurt by any means except
damno fatali, or by inevitable accident; and even
then Ulpian intimates that innkeepers were not altogether restrained from knavish practices or suspicious neglect." [1]

"Still," said the by-stander aforesaid, "I do not
see how the reticule can be considered to have been
under our landlord's care."

"To render him liable it is not necessary that the
goods be placed in his special keeping, or brought
to his special notice. If they be in the inn, brought
there in an ordinary and reasonable way by a guest,
it is sufficient to charge the proprietor." [2]

"Yes," I chimed in, "and it does not matter in
what part of the hotel the goods are kept, whether
'up-stairs, or down-stairs, or in the lady's chamber':
while they are anywhere within it, they are under
the care of Boniface, and he is responsible for their
safe custody. He is equally liable, whether baggage is put in a bedroom, a horse handed over to
the care of the hostler,[3] or goods placed in an out-

[1] Wharton on Innkeepers, p. 88.
[2] Cayle's Case; Packard *v.* Northcraft, 2 Met. (Ky.) 439;
Norcross *v.* Norcross, 53 Me. 163; Burrows *v.* Truber, 21 Md.
320; McDonald *v.* Edgerton, 5 Barb. 560; Coykendall *v.* Eaton, 55 Barb. 188.
[3] Hallenbake *v.* Fish, 8 Wend. 547.

house belonging to the establishment and used for that sort of articles.1 My friend Epps, on one occasion, went to an inn down in Mississippi, and had his trunk taken to his bedroom, and it being broken into at night and the money purloined, the innkeeper was held liable."2

"A friend of mine," said the English gent, "who was in the employ of a sweet fellow of the name of Candy, on arriving at an inn gave his luggage to Boots, who placed one package in the hall; afterwards the servant wished to carry it into the commercial room, but the owner requested him to leave it where it was; the parcel mysteriously disappeared, and the innkeeper had the pleasure of paying for it."3

"In fact, I believe an innkeeper cannot make his guest take care of his own goods;4 nor is a traveler bound to deposit his valuables in the hotel safe, even though he may know that there is one kept for the reception of such articles, and there is a regulation of the house requiring articles of value to be so deposited,"5 I remarked.

"Are you not stating that rather broadly?" questioned my legal confrere.

"No Vatican Council has proclaimed me infallible. I know full well that when the poet said 'to err is human,' he spoke truth. Of course, I am

1 Chute v. Wiggins, 14 Johns. 175.

2 Epps v. Hinds, 27 Miss. 657; Simon v. Miller, 7 La. An. 368.

8 Candy v. Spencer, 3 Fost. & F. 306.

4 Bennett v. Mellor, 5 Term. Rep. 273.

5 Johnson v. Richardson, 17 Ill. 302; Piper v. Hall, 14 La. An. 324; Profilet v. Hall, Ibid. 524.

speaking only of the rule in States in which there is no special law or statute on the point, limiting the liability of publicans," I replied.

"I think, however," said Mr. Inthelaw, the Englishman, "that it has been held that the inn-keeper may refuse to be responsible for the safe custody of the guest's goods unless they are put in a certain place, and if the guest objects to this, the host will be exonerated in case of loss.[1] And a guest who has actual notice of a regulation of the inn as to the deposit of valuables, and has not complied with it, takes the risk of loss happening from any cause, except, of course, the actual sins of omission and commission of the landlord or his servants."[2]

"And very reasonably," remarked a by-stander.

"But clear and unmistakable notice of these regulations restricting the publican's liability must certainly be given,"[3] I asserted. "And," I continued, "I believe a distinction has been taken, and it appears to rest upon good reason, between those effects of a traveler not immediately requisite to his comfort, and those essential to his personal convenience, and which it is necessary that he should have constantly about him; so that, though personally notified, he is not bound to deposit the latter with the innkeeper.

[1] Saunders *v.* Spencer, Dyer, 266*a*; Wilson *v.* Halpin, 30 How. Pr. 124; Packard *v.* Northcraft, 2 Met. (Ky.) 439; Fuller *v.* Coats, 18 Ohio St. 343.

[2] Stanton *v.* Leland, 4 E. D. Smith, 88; Kellogg *v.* Sweeney, 1 Lans. N. Y. 397.

[3] Van Wyck *v.* Howard, 12 How. Pr. 147.

And, perhaps, this distinction will explain the apparently contradictory decisions."[1]

"Doubtless the notice must be clear. Even a printed notification is not sufficient. It must be brought home to the mind of the guest, or at least to his knowledge, before he enters and takes possession of his room, so that, if he does not like the regulations, he may go elsewhere.[2] In one case, the register was headed with the notice, 'Money and valuables, it is agreed, shall be placed in the safe in the office; otherwise, the proprietor will not be liable for loss'; and Mr. Bernstein duly entered his name in the book; still he was not held bound by the notice, as there was no proof that it was seen or assented to by him."[3]

By-stander here remarked: "My father kept an inn in New York State, and once told a man of the name of Purvis, when he arrived at the house, that there was a safe for valuables, and that he would not be responsible for his unless they were placed in it. Purvis, however, neglected the caution, and left $2,000 in gold in a trunk in his bed-room, locked the door, and gave the key to my father. Some thief broke through and stole, and Purvis tried to make the old gentleman responsible for the theft; but the court did not agree with him, and considered that he alone must bear the loss."[4]

[1] Profilet v. Hall, 16 La. An. 524.

[2] Morgan v. Ravey, 30 L. J. Exch. 131, per Wilde, B.; 6 Hurl. & N. 265.

[3] Bernstein v. Sweeny, 33 N. Y. Sup. Ct. 271. See, also, Kent v. Midland Rwy. L. R. 10 Q. B. 1; Henderson v. Stevenson, L. R. 2 Scotch & D. 470.

[4] Purvis v. Coleman. 21 N. Y. 111.

"The host is not liable for the loss of goods if, at the time of their disappearance, they were in the exclusive possession of their owner,[1] and it will generally be left to an intelligent jury to say whether or not the articles were in the sole custody of the guest,"[2] remarked Mr. Inthelaw.

"What do you mean?" asked one.

"For instance, where a Brummagem man, traveling for orders, came to an inn with three boxes of goods; the travelers' room did not meet with his approbation, so he asked for another one up stairs, where he might display his wares. The lady of the house gave him one with a key in the door, and told him to keep it locked. The boxes were taken to the new apartment, and after dining in the t: veiers' room, the Brummagem gent—who seemed inclined to put on airs—took his precious self into the new room, and there also he took his wine. After his repast, he exhibited his wares—chiefly jewelry—to a customer, and in the cool of the evening went out to see the town, leaving the door unlocked, and the key outside. (So the reporter tells us, though why he need have taken the trouble to leave the door unlocked if the key was on the outside, or the key outside if the door was unlocked, I cannot understand.) While he was away, two of his boxes went away, too. He sued the proprietor of the house for damages, but got nothing. He applied for a new trial, but with like success. Lord

---

[1] Farnsworth v. Packwood, 1 Stark. 249; Packard v. Northcraft, 2 Met. (Ky.) 439; Vance v. Throckmorton, 5 Bush, (Ky.) 41.

[2] Farnsworth v. Packwood, *supra*.

Ellenborough remarked that it seemed to him that
the care of the goods in a room used for the exhibi-
tion of the goods to persons over whom the innkeeper could have no check or control hardly fell
within the limits of his duty as an innkeeper; that
the room was not merely intrusted to our friend in
the ordinary character of a guest frequenting an
inn, but that he must be understood as having
special charge of it. And another learned judge
gave it as his sentiments that the traveler should be
taken to have received the favor of the private
room *cum onere ;* that is, he accepted it upon the
condition of taking the goods under his own care." [1]

"But," I said, "of course, simply ordering goods
to be placed in a particular room is not such a taking under one's own care as to absolve an innkeeper
from his responsibility.[2]   I recollect a case where a
traveler, on arriving, requested his *impedimenta*, as
old Cæsar used to say, to be taken to the commercial room; they were, and they were stolen, and
the innkeeper was held bound to recoup the man,
although he proved that the usual practice of the
house was to place the luggage in the guest's room,
and not in the commercial room, unless an express
order was given to the contrary. The chief justice
remarked that if mine host had intended not to be
responsible unless his guests chose to have their
goods placed in their sleeping apartments, or such
other place as to him might seem meet, he should
have told them so." [3]

[1] Burgess *v.* Clements, 4 Maule & S. 307.
[2] Packard *v.* Northcraft, 2 Met. (Ky.) 439.
[3] Richmond *v.* Smith, 8 Barn. & C. 9.

By-stander observed that the law seemed inconsistent, as there did not appear to be much difference between the two cases.

"Mr. Justice Holroyd distinguished the latter from the former case by saying that the Birmingham man asked to have a room which he used for the purposes of trade, not merely as a guest in the inn.[1] In Wisconsin, it was held that the retention by a guest of money or valuables upon his person was not such exclusive control as to exonerate an innkeeper from liability, if the loss was not induced by the negligence or misconduct of the guest,"[2] remarked one who knew whereof he affirmed.

"An hotel-keeper is of course liable for the conduct of another guest, placed in a room already occupied, without the consent of the occupant.[3] And where a guest left his door unlocked, because he was told that he must either do so or get up in the night and open it, as others had to share the room with him, the innkeeper was held liable for everything lost."[4]

This very learned and intensely uninteresting discussion was here summarily put a stop to by the appearance in the room of several ladies who had respectively claims upon the respective talkers, and who were ready and willing to inspect the inside of the luncheon hall.

"How singularly our hours of refection have changed," remarked Mr. L. Inthelaw. "You re-

---

[1] Richmond v. Smith, 8 Barn. & C. 9.
[2] Jailei v. Cardinal, 35 Wis. 118.
[3] Dessauer v. Baker, 1 Wilson (Ind.) 429.
[4] Milford v. Wesley, 1 Wilson (Ind.) 119.

member that in the sixteenth century the saying was:

'Lever à cinq, diner à neuf,
Souper à cinq, coucher à neuf,
Fait vivre d'ans nonante et neuf.'

"And even in the early days of the reign of Louis XIV the dinner hour of the court was eleven o'clock, or noon at the latest."

"Yes," I replied, "I have noticed that the his-torians say that one of the causes which hastened the death of Louis XII was his changing his dinner hour from nine to twelve at the solicitation of his wife. What a fine house this is!"

"Well, sir," was the response, "believe a stranger and a foreigner when he tells you that, good as are some of the hotels in Europe, the American ones surpass them all both in size and in general fitness of purpose."

"I am glad to hear you say so. I presume that the great extent of our territory, the natural dispo-sition of our people to travel, our extensive network of railways, have developed our hotel system, and made it, as you say, without a parallel in the world," I replied.

"Have you traveled much, sir?" asked Mrs. Lawyer.

"Yes, well nigh all round the world. And so, I flatter myself, I have had more experience in hotels than most men."

"You must have seen a great variety," I re-marked.

The Englishman smilingly replied: "In far off China I have carried about my own bedding from inn to inn, not caring to occupy that in which a Celestial, a Tartar, or a Russian had slept the night before. In France, I have taken around my little piece of soap, an almost unknown luxury in Continental hotels. In India, I have lodged in the dak bungalows provided by the government, where the articles of furniture are like donkey's gallops—few and far between. There you must manage the commissariat department yourself if you would not starve. I remember once stopping at one of the best country hotels in the Bombay Presidency, and was given a sitting-room, a bed-room, and a bath-room; but in the first a number of birds had built their nests, and flew in and out and roundabout at their pleasure; in the bed-room a colony of ants swarmed over the floor, while in my third room cockroaches and other creeping things gave a variegated hue to the pavement; everything else was in keeping."

"Horrors!" exclaimed Mrs. L.

"Unpleasant, to say the least," I remarked, "unless, indeed, you were a naturalist."

"I think," continued our traveled friend, "that one never feels at home in an European hotel. You never know your landlord or your fellow-sojourners; the *table d'hôte* in the grand dining-halls prevents all intercourse between the guests; they never have a smoking-room, a billiard-room, a bar-room, or a bath-room; if you want to do 'tumbies' you are furnished with a regular old tub."

"I know that from experience," said my wife. "Once at a grand hotel in Florence I wanted a bath, and was promised one. By-and-by, as I sat at my window in the gloaming, I saw a man trundling a handcart containing a bath and some barrels. In a few minutes two men solemnly ushered this identical tub into my room, then in three successive trips they brought in three barrels of water, two cold, the other hot; a sheet was spread over the bath, and the water allowed to gurgle out of the bunghole into it, while with uprolled sleeve the swarthy Italian mingled the hot and the cold with his hand till what he considered a suitable temperature was gained. When all was ready, the man coolly asked how soon he should come back for his apparatus. Actually there was neither bath nor water in the hotel, although the Arno rolled beneath its windows. As you say, bath-rooms are unknown in civilized Europe."

"Then, again," I said, "if you want your dinner, and are not at *table d'hôte*, you must write out a list of what you want as long as a newspaper editorial, hand it in, and wait longer than it would take to set it up in type before the eatables appear. I have known people wait an hour at swell hotels, and then go away unsatisfied."

"There are plenty of hotels in all large English towns," said our friend; "but none a quarter of the size of the large caravansaries to be found in New York, Philadelphia, Chicago, or San Francisco. Their exteriors are rather fine, a few rooms are well furnished; but, on the whole, they are dark and dingy."

"Were you ever at the Grand Hôtel du Louvre, in Paris?" asked my wife.

"Yes. What a splendid place it is! The dining-room is not the largest, but it is as fine as any in the world; its ornamentation is so chaste, its chandeliers so splendid, its mirrors so magnificent, and the dinner is perfection; in fact, as some one says, it is the elysium of the *bon-vivants* and the paradise of the esthetic. But if I go on in this style you will take me for a 'runner' for first-class hotels." We then passed on to another subject, as the reader must to another chapter.

Chapter IV.

GUESTS, WAGERS, AND GAMES.

A fashionable young gent—a dweller in the city —(on whose face nature, as in the case of the Honorable Percy Popjoy, had burst out with a chin-tuft, but, exhausted with the effort, had left the rest of the countenance smooth as an infant's cheek) had been enjoying himself with some kindred spirits, (and some spirits far stronger, too,) and being belated, as well as rather bewildered, with the potations of the evening, went to bed in our hotel. The next morning he found himself the possessor of a splitting headache, but minus his gold repeater; so he kindly and condescendingly consulted me upon the subject of the proprietor's liability to make good his loss.

I told him that in my opinion he had better save up his money and buy a new watch, for there were several reasons why the hotel-keeper need not give him one.

"What are they?" he asked.

"We need not consider," I replied, "the question of your negligence in carelessly exhibiting your watch among a lot of people at the bar, nor in leaving your door unlocked, nor need we say that because your intoxication contributed to the loss, therefore the landlord is not liable.[1] The fact

---

[1] Walsh v. Porterfield, Sup. Ct. Pa. 19 Alb. L. J. 376.

that you were not a traveler is sufficient to prevent your recovering. Long since it was laid down in old Bacon that inns are for passengers and wayfaring men, so that a friend or a neighbor can have no action as a guest against the landlord."[1]

"What in thunder have I to do with what is laid down in old Bacon?"

"What is to be found inside old Bacon, and old calf, and old sheep, has a good deal to do with every one who makes an old pig of himself," I testily replied.

"I trust, sir, that you use that last epithet in its Pickwickian sense," said the young exquisite.

"Certainly, certainly," I hastened to reply, "if you will so accept it."

"Then I would ask," continued my interrogator, "must a man be a certain length of time at an hotel before he is entitled to the privileges of a guest?"

"Oh, dear, no! Merely purchasing temporary refreshment at an inn makes the purchaser a guest and renders the innkeeper liable for the safety of the goods he may have with him,[2] if he is a traveler."

"But who is a traveler?"

"One who is absent from his home, whether on pleasure or business.[3] A townsman or neighbor, who is actually traveling, may be a guest.[4] In a

[1] Bacon, Abridg., vol. 4, p. 448.

[2] McDonald v. Edgerton, 5 Barb. 560; Bennett v. Mellor, 5 T. R. 274.

[3] Per Cockburn, C. J., Atkinson v. Sellars, 5 C. B. N. S. 442.

[4] Walling v. Potter, 35 Conn. 183.

New York case, where a resident of the town left his horses at the inn stables, it was decided that the proprietor was not liable for them.[1] So if a ball is given at an hotel the guests present cannot hold the proprietor liable for any losses occurring while they are tripping the light fantastic toe, as he did not receive them in his public capacity." [2]

" But," remarked a person standing by, " but how would it be if a traveler left his baggage at an hotel and stopped elsewhere ? "

" If one leaves any dead thing, as baggage, at an inn he will not be considered a guest; [3] if, on the other hand, he leaves a horse, he becomes entitled to all the privileges and immunities of a guest, even though he himself lodges elsewhere." [4]

" Why the difference ? " quoth one.

" I might, perhaps, be more correct if I said that on this point the authorities are antagonistic.[5] The distinction, however, was made because, as the horse must be fed, the innkeeper has a profit out of it, whereas he gets nothing out of a dead thing.[6] One need not, however, take all his meals or lodge every night at the inn where his baggage is. It is sufficient if he takes a room and lodges or boards at the house part of the time." [7]

[1] Grinnell v. Cook, 3 Hill, (N. Y.) 486.
[2] Carter v. Hobbs, 12 Mich. 52.
[3] Gelley v. Clarke, Cro. Jac. 188; Orange Co. Bank v. Brown, 9 Wend. 114.
[4] York v. Grindstone, 1 Salk. 388 ; Mason v. Thompson, 9 Pick. 280; Peet v. McGraw, 25 Wend. 653.
[5] Ingalsbee v. Woods, 33 N. Y. 577; Parsons on Contracts, vol. 2, p. 153.
[6] York v. Grindstone, *supra*.
[7] McDaniels v. Robinson, 26 Vt. 316.

"I think I have heard that if one makes an agreement for boarding by the week, he ceases to have the rights of a guest," said the previous speaker.

"The length of time for which a person resides at an hotel does not affect his rights, so long as he retains his transient character;[1] nor does he cease to be a guest by proposing after his arrival to remain a certain time, nor by his ascertaining the charges, nor by paying in advance, nor from time to time as his wants are supplied,[2] nor even by arranging to pay so much a week for his board, if he stays so long, after he has taken up his quarters at the house;[3] but if when he first arrives he makes a special agreement as to board,[4] or for the use of a room,[5] he never becomes a guest, and the innkeeper's liability is totally different, being only that of an ordinary bailee. One visiting a boarder at an inn is a guest, and the keeper is liable for the loss of his goods, though not of the boarder's."[6]

"And when does a person cease to have the rights of a guest?" again queried the questioner.

I replied, "An innkeeper's liability, as such, ceases when the guest pays his bill and quits the house with the declared intention of not returning,

---

[1] Parkhurst v. Foster, Sal. 388.
[2] Pinkerton v. Woodward, 33 Cal. 557.
[3] Shoecraft v. Bailey, 25 Iowa, 553 ; Berkshire Woollen Co. v. Proctor, 7 Cush. 417 ; Hall v. Pike, 100 Mass. 495.
[4] Chamberlain v. Masterson, 26 Ala. 371 ; Manning v. Wells, 9 Humph. 746; Ewart v. Stark, 8 Rich. 423; Hursh v. Beyers, 29 Mo. 469; Parkhurst v. Foster, Sal. 388.
[5] Parker v. Flint, 12 Mod. 255.
[6] Lusk v. Belote, 22 Minn. 468.

and if he then leaves any of his possessions behind him, the landlord is no longer liable for their safe keeping, unless he has taken special charge of them, and then only as any other common bailee would be.[1]   And this appears to be so, even when an arrangement has been made for the keep of the guest's horse.[2]   Unless specially authorized, a clerk cannot bind his master by an agreement to keep safely a guest's baggage after he leaves."[3]

" But supposing one pays his bills and goes off expecting to have his traps sent after him immediately to the station?" questioned a new interrogator.

" Mrs. Clark went to 'The Exchange Hotel' in Atlanta, with eight trunks; on leaving, the porter of the inn took charge of the baggage, promising to deliver it for her at the cars. He lost two of the pieces, and it was held that the liability of the hotel-keeper continued until such delivery was actually made.[4]   On the same principle that when an innkeeper sends his porter to the cars to receive the baggage of intending guests, he is responsible until it is actually re-delivered into the custody of the guests.   And where a man paid his bill for the whole day and went off, leaving his trunk, with twenty cents for porterage, to be sent to the boat, the innkeeper was held liable until the baggage was actually put on board.[5]   The liability for bag-

---

[1] Wintermate v. Clarke, 5 Sandf. 262; Lawrence v. Howard, 1 Utah T. 142.

[2] McDaniels v. Robinson, 28 Vt. 387.

[3] Corkindale v. Eaton, 40 How. N. Y. Pr. 266.

[4] Sasseen v. Clark, 37 Ga. 242.

[5] Giles v. Fauntleroy, 13 Md. 126.

gage left with an innkeeper with his consent, continues for a reasonable time after the settlement of the bill, and even after a reasonable time he is responsible for gross negligence.[1] Where a visitor had actual notice that the landlord would not be responsible for valuables unless put under his care, and on preparing to depart gave a trunk containing precious goods into the care of the servants and it was lost, yet the innkeeper was held liable.[2] So, also, where valuables were stolen from a trunk after the guest had packed it, locked his room, and given notice of his departure, and delivered the key of his room to the clerk to have the trunk brought down.[3] What is all that row about?"

Weary of the conversation, and being attracted by some rather loud conversation in another part of the room, I walked off to see what it was all about, and soon found that it was anent a young lady's age.

" I bet you she is—" began one of the disputants.

"Stop!" I cried, "that is not a proper wager."

"Begad! what do you mean, sir?" was queried in tones not the mildest.

" Simply that where a wager concerns the person of another, no action can be maintained upon it. As Buller, J., once remarked, a bet on a lady's age, or whether she has a mole on her face, is void. No person has a right to make it a subject of discussion in a court of justice, whether she passes herself in

---

[1] Adams v. Clenn, 41 Ga. 65.
[2] Stanton v. Leland, 4 E. D. Smith, 88.
[3] Bendetson v. French, 46 N. Y. 266; Kellogg v. Sweeney, Ibid. 291.

the world to be more in the bloom of youth than
she really is, or whether what is apparent to every
one who sees her, is a mole or a wart; although a
lady cannot bring an action against a man for saying she is thirty-three when she passes for only
twenty-three, nor for saying she has a wart on her
face. Nor will the courts try a wager as to whether a
young lady squints with her right eye or with her
left.[1] And Lord Mansfield came to very much the
same conclusion in discussing the law in a celebrated
wager case concerning the gender of a certain individual,[2] because, as his lordship remarked, actions
on such wagers would disturb the peace of individ-
uals and society."

"Confound it, the fellow seems to have swallowed
a law library," muttered one man; while another
said,

" But surely many wagers equally as absurd have
been sued on in courts of law with success."

" There is no doubt of that," I replied. " It was
done upon a bet of 'six to four that Bob Booby
would win the plate at the New Lichfield races;'[3]
also, upon a wager of a 'rump and dozen' whether
one of the betters were older than the other.[4] In
the latter case the C. J. modestly said that he did
not judicially know what a 'rump and dozen'
meant; but another judge more candidly remarked
that privately he knew that it meant a good dinner
and wine. And a bet as to whose father would die

[1] Good v. Elliott, 3 T. R. 693.
[2] Da Costa v. Jones, Cowper, 729.
[3] McAllister v. Haden, 2 Campb. 436.
[4] Hussey v. Crickett, 3 Campb. 160.

first was held good, although one old man was de-
funct at the time, the fact not being known to the
parties.[1]   But Lord Ellenborough refused to try
an action on a wager on a cock-fight." [2]

"Although at common law many wagers were
legal," remarked the English gentleman alluded to
aforetime, "still, in England, as the law now stands,
all wagers are null and void at law,[3] and if the loser
either cannot or won't pay, the law will not assist
the winner;[4] but either party may recover the
stake deposited by him, before it is paid over to
the winner by the holder.   That point was settled
in the case of a genius who bet all the philosophers,
divines, and scientific professors in the United
Kingdom, £500, that they could not prove the ro-
tundity and revolution of the earth from Scripture,
from reason, or from fact, the wager to be won by
the taker if he could exhibit to the satisfaction of
an intelligent referee a convex railway, canal, or
lake." [5]

"Was the referee satisfied?" asked a bystander.

"Yes; it was proved to his satisfaction that on a
canal, in a distance of six miles, there was a curva-
ture to and fro of five feet, more or less.   And then
the man asked his stake back, and got it, too."

"In New York," I said, "it has been held, under
a statute giving the losing party a right of action
against the stake-holder for the stake, whether the

[1] Earl of March v. Pigot, 5 Burr. 2802.
[2] Squires v. Whisken, 3 Camp. 140.
[3] See 8 and 9 Vict., chap. 109.
[4] Savage v. Madden, 36 L. J. Ex. 178.
[5] Hampden v. Walsh, L. R. 1 Q. B. Div. 189.

stake has been paid over by the stake-holder or not, and whether the wager be lost or not, that the holder is liable to the loser, although he had paid over the stake by his directions.[1] And in several of the States, if the wager is illegal, the stake-holder is liable to be made refund the stakes, notwithstanding payment to the winner."[2]

"Such decisions are subversive of all honor and honesty," said a betting looking character.

"Not so. A bet should be a contract of honor, and no more. One should not bet unless he can trust his opponent. The time of the courts of law should not be taken up by such matters."

"Are the American courts as hard upon wagers as the English?" asked the Englishman.

"Quite so," I replied. "In some parts of the country they have been prohibited by statute, and some courts have denied them any validity whatever. In Colorado it was held that the courts had enough to do without devoting their time to the solution of questions arising out of idle bets made on dog and cock-fights, horse-races, the speed of trains, the construction of railroads, the number on a dice, or the character of a card that may be turned up.[3] Even if admitted to be valid in any case, it is quite clear upon the authorities that they cannot be upheld where they refer to the person or property of another, so as to make him infamous or

[1] Ruchman v. Pitcher, 1 Comst. 392.
[2] Garrison v. McGregor, 51 Ill. 473; Adkins v. Fleming, 29 Iowa, 122; Searle v. Prevost, 4 Houst. (Del.) 467. But see Johnston v. Russell, 37 Cal. 670.
[3] Eldred v. Malloy, 2 Col. 320.

to injure him, or if they are libelous, or indecent, or tend to break the peace.[1] In some States it has been decided that wagers upon the result of elections are against public policy, and therefore void. In California, during the presidential campaign of 1868, a man called Johnson bet that Horatio Seymour would have a majority of votes in that State, while one Freeman bet that U. S. Grant would be the lucky man. Mr. Russell was the stakeholder. After the result of the election was known, Johnson demanded his money back, but Russell honorably paid it over to the winner; so J. turned round and sued for it. The Court held, that if Johnson had repudiated his bet and asked for his money before the election, or before the result was known, he might have got it, but that now he was too late.[2] Judge Sanderson remarked that in times of political excitement persons might be provoked to make wagers which they might regret in their cooler moments. No obstacles, he thought, should be thrown in the way of their repentance, and if they retracted before the bet has been decided, their money ought to be returned; but those who allow their stakes to remain until after the wager has been decided and the result known, are entitled to no such consideration; their tears, if any, are not repentant tears, but such as crocodiles shed over the victims they are about to devour."[3]

"Ah, then it has been judicially decided that

---

[1] Parsons on Contracts, vol. 2, p. 756.
[2] Yates v. Foot, 12 Johns. 1.
[3] Johnson v. Russell, 37 Cal. 670.

crocodiles weep," sarcastically observed a by-
stander.

From talking on wagering, we naturally passed
to the subject of gaming—a kindred vice.

"I believe that in England there is a law forbid-
ding an innkeeper to allow any gaming on his premises," I remarked.

"Yes," said the English barrister. "Any licensed
innkeeper who suffers any gaming or betting or
unlawful games upon his premises, runs the risk of
being fined."[1]

"What do they consider gaming?" asked a rak-
ish looking individual, who seemed as if he understood practically what it was.

"Playing at any game for money,[2] or beer,
or money's worth;[3] or even exhibiting betting
lists."[4]

"That seems precious hard," quoth the rake.

"In one case an innkeeper was punished for allowing his own private friends to play at cards for
money in his own private room, on the licensed
premises."[5]

"Not much liberty in England," remarked the
youth.

"That was almost as bad as the tavernkeeper
who was fined by some energetic Yorkshire magis-

[1] Wharton on Innkeepers, 62.

[2] Rex v. Ashton, 22 L. J. M. C. 1.

[3] Danford v. Taylor, 22 L. T. Rep. 483 ; Foot v. Baker, 6
Scott N. R. 301.

[4] Searle v. St. Martins' J. J. 4 J. P. 276 ; Avards v. Dunce,
26 J. P. 437.

[5] Patten v. Rhymer, 29 L. J. M. C. 189.

trate for being drunk in his own bed, in his own house!"[1] observed another.

"Farewell to the fond notion that an Englishman's house is his castle!" melodramatically exclaimed the youth.

"But please allow me to say that Lust, J., held, in a very recent case, that although an innkeeper, if drunk on his own premises while they are open, is as much amenable to the penalty as if he was found drunk upon the highway, yet it could never have been intended that an innkeeper who is drunk in his own bedroom should be liable any more than a person—not a publican—found drunk in his own private house,"[2] said the Englishman.

"And what, pray, may be the unlawful games which are so strictly forbidden inside the tavern— the poor man's home?" asked the youth.

"Dice, ace of hearts, faro, basset, hazard, passage, or any game played with dice, or with any instrument, engine, or device in the nature of dice, having figures or numbers thereon, and roulette, or rolly-polly; and bull-baiting, bear-baiting, badger-baiting, dog-fighting, cock-fighting, and all such games, are unlawful," replied the Englishman.

"Surely, you have not got through the black list yet," ironically remarked our rake.

"Those mentioned, and the game of puff and dart, if played for money or money's worth,[3] and lotteries and sweepstakes, except in cases of art unions, where works of art are given as prizes, are

[1] Wharton, 81.
[2] Lester v. Torrens, L. R. 2 Q. B. Div. 403.
[3] Bew v. Harston, L. R. 3 Q. B. Div. 454.

all the games I remember, that are prohibited by
the Statutes of Henry VIII, George II, and her
present Majesty."

"May I ask what games you are permitted to indulge in? I do not see that any are left, except the
'grinning through a halter,' spoken of in *The Spec-
tator*, in which highly intellectual and moral con-
test the rule is

> "'The dreadfullest grinner
> To be the winner.'

"Backgammon and all games played upon backgammon boards,[1] quoits, tennis, and all games of
mere skill, are perfectly lawful, unless played for
money or money's worth."[2]

"And what of billiards?"

"Oh, that is not unlawful unless played for
money."[3]

"No wonder," said Mr. Rake, "that people emi-
grate from that benighted land. And yet Henry
VII, and James I, and his estimable son, Prince
Henry, were remarkably fond of having a game of
cards; although Scotch Jamie was so lazy a coon
that he required a servant to hold his hand for him.
I believe that those good sovereigns who passed
these virtuous laws took care to except from their
operation their royal palaces."[4]

"I would remind you, my good sir," I said, "that
gaming is forbidden in almost all the States; that

[1] 13 Geo. II, chap. 19.
[2] 8 and 9 Vict. chap. 109. sec. 1.
[3] Wharton, 65.
[4] Abinger, C. B., in McKinnell *v.* Robinson, 3 M. & W. 430

a judge in South Carolina said that if he could
have his own way, he would hold that a billiard
room kept for filthy lucre's sake was a nuisance at
common law;[1] and the same judge decided that a
bowling-alley kept for gain was a nuisance. In
Kentucky, it was held unlawful to throw dice to see
who should pay for the drinks;[2] in Virginia, betting on a game of bagatelle was held illegal;[3]
while in Tennessee, selling prize-candy packages
was decided to be gaming and indictable."[4]

"Alas, my country!"

"By the way, do you remember, sir, the distinction the Ettrick Shepherd drew between the card-
playing of old people and that of young folk?"
asked an elderly bystander of Scotian descent.

"No, what was it?"

"He says, 'you'll generally fin' that auld folk
that play carrds have been raither freevolous, and
no muckle addicteed to thocht, unless they're
greedy, and play for the pool, which is fearsome in
auld age. But as for young folks, lads and lasses
like, when the gude man and his wife are gaen to
bed, what's the harm in a gaem at cairds? It's a
cheerfu' noisy sicht o' comfort and confusion; sic
lookin' into ane ainither's han's! sic fause shufflin'!
sic unfair dealin'! sic winkin' to tell your pairtner
that ye hae the king or the ace! And when that
winna do, sic kicken' o' shins an' treadin' on taes

---

[1] Tanner v. Albion, 5 Hill, 128 ; but see People v. Sargeant,
8 Cowen, 139.

[2] McDaniels v. Commonwealth, 6 Bush. 326.

[3] Neal's Case, 22 Gratt. 917.

[4] Eubanks v. State, 3 Hersk. 488.

aneath the table—often the wrong anes! Then what gigglin' amang the lasses! what amiable, nay, love quarrels between pairtners! jokin' an' jeestin', and tauntin' an' toozlin'—the cawnel blawn out, an' the sound of a thousan' kisses. That's caird-playin' in the kintra, Mr. North, and where's the man amang ye that 'll daur to say that it's no' a pleasant pastime o' a winter nicht, when the snaw is a cumin' doon the hun, or the speat's roarin' amang the mirk mountains?"

"Give us that in English," said the forward young man, as he left the room.

*   *   *   *   *

There was a door between our bedroom and that adjoining. Upon taking possession, we tried it; it appeared fast, but the key was not on our side and the bolt was *hors du combat.*

My wife had retired for the night, and was rapidly approaching that moment when the rustling silk, the embroidered skirt, the pannier, the braids, and elaborately arranged coiffure are exchanged for a *robe de nuit* of virgin white and a bob of hair on the head, *simplex numditiis.* Suddenly the door between the two rooms creaked, squeaked, and opened, and a creature clad in man's attire protruded his head. When, however, he saw that the room was occupied he drew back, laughing to himself as he locked the door.

On my arrival I found the partner of my joys and sorrows perched upon the bed like Patience on a monument. Immediately chambermaids, housemaids, and waiters were summoned, and informed that the key must be taken out of that dreadful door and placed in the office. After his voyage of discovery, Paul Pry had gone out, so a waiter entered the room, took the key, and having hampered the lock of P. P.'s door, he passed out *via* our room, my wife gracefully retiring into a closet. When we were quietly reclining on our downy couch we heard our neighbor making fruitless efforts to regain his room; in vain he summoned the chambermaid with her keys; in vain came the waiter with his. P. P. had to pass the night in another apartment, minus his toilet appointments.

"What would I have done," asked my wife, "if that horrid wretch had come into the room?"

"Oh, we could have brought an action of trespass against him;[1] for the possession we have of this room is quite sufficient to entitle us to recover against a wrong-doer, although we could not maintain such an action against the hotel-keeper if he should enter for any proper purpose."[2]

"But that would not be a very great satisfaction," said my wife.

"Well, it is the best we could do, for we could not summon to our aid the good spirits that interfered on behalf of the Lady Godiva to punish Peeping Tom."

"But what if he had assaulted me?" she queried.

"Well, I am afraid I would have had to settle the matter with him, for an innkeeper is not bound

[1] Graham *v.* Peat, 1 East, 246.
[2] Doyle *v.* Walker, 26 U C. R. 502.

7.

to keep safe the bodies of his guests,[1] but merely their baggage; that is, such articles of necessary or personal convenience as are usually carried by travelers for their own use, the facts and circumstances of each case deciding what these articles may be.[2] Hush! what is that?"

"A mosquito."

"Well, I must kill it."

"Never mind," urged my wife. "Spare the little creature."

"I can't stand their bites any more than my betters, and others who have gone before. When they pierced the boots of the Father of his Country in the New Jersey marshes, that exemplary individual indulged in bad language; they drove back the army of Julian the Apostate, or apostle, as Lord Kenyon called him; they compelled Sapor, the Persian, to raise the siege of Nisibes, stinging his elephants and camels into madness; they render some parts of the banks of the Po uninhabitable, and cause people in some countries to sleep in pits with nothing but their heads above ground. How, then, can you expect me to lie quietly here and wait to have their horrid war-whoop sung in mine ears, as they dance in giddy mazes from side to side, ere they plunge their sharp stilettos into my shrinking flesh?"

Forthwith I arose, lit the gas, and wandered round and round the room, a white-stoled acolyte of science, with a towel in my hand, ready to take

[1] Cayle's Case, 8 Co. 32.
[2] Lasseen v. Clark, 37 Ga. 242.

the life of any member of the extensive family of *Culex Pipiens.* Long was the search after the tireless musician, blowing his own trumpet as enthusiastically as any other musical genius. My wife mocked me as I danced about, flipping to the right and to the left; but at last Mrs. Mosquito, swanlike, sang a song, which (to me, at least) was her sweetest, as it was her last.

CHAPTER V.

SAFES AND BAGGAGE.

Shortly after this, while traveling in a palace car, and during the night, Mrs. Lawyer lost some of her paraphernalia, and felt strongly inclined to make a row about it; but I quoted the sublime words of somebody or other, "Let us have peace," and then told her that the owners of sleeping cars—who receive pay in advance from travelers merely for the sleeping accommodations afforded by their cars, and this only from a particular class of persons, and for a particular berth, and for a particular trip—are not liable as innkeepers for money or property that may be stolen from the lodgers on their cars; and that, as they only furnish sleeping accommodation for travelers who have already paid the railway company—over whose line the cars run—for their transportation, and receive no part of the fare paid for transportation, they are not common carriers, nor are they liable for property lost or stolen from their carriages. Mr. Chester M. Smith, who lost $1,180 on the Pullman car "Missouri," in the State of Illinois, in December, 1872, was the innocent cause of the enunciation of the law upon this point. The court held that a Pullman car is not a common inn—that it does not accommodate persons indiscriminately—does not furnish victual and lodging, but only lodging — affords no accommodation but a berth and bed, and a place and conveniences for toilet purposes—does not receive pay for caring, nor undertake to care, for the goods of travelers; but the accommodation afforded is the result of an express contract, and that the liabilities of innkeepers should not be extended to others.[1]

We had passed from one State into another, and had now taken up our quarters at a magnificent hotel (its name will not be mentioned, for I do not desire to injure any of the other houses). As we stepped out of the cab, we entered a vast and handsome office of white marble, and passed up to the splendid parlors and luxurious bed-rooms above. The way I wrote our names in the register, and asked for dinner in our private sitting-room, led the gentlemanly clerk to believe that myself and Mrs. Lawyer had but lately entered into a partnership for weal and woe; this I found when the elegantly attired waiters served our dinner. The whole service was one continued tribute to Love. On the soup tureen were little Cupids, training a huge turtle; on the fish plates, as mermaids and mermen, they were riding on salmon and dolphins; on the other dishes, these naked little rascals flew about among beautiful birds, hid under strawberry vines, or swung in spider-web hammocks from sprays of wild blackberry; they dug in ravines like mountain gnomes, and pried and lifted carrots with comical machinery, as though they were great bars and ingots of yellow gold. Some of the dish-covers were shaped like cabbages, and Cupids peeped from under every

---

[1] Pullman Palace Car Co. v. Smith, 73 Ill. 360.

curling leaf; others, again, gathered the vintage and trod the grapes. Last of all, on the dessert service was represented the marriage of the queen of the flower fairies, each piece a different flower, with a love perched on it, some with torches, others with instruments of music; while the central stand represented the ceremony itself; a scarlet cardinal-flower was saying mass, and on the highest point of the dish, (which represented a church tower,) a chorus of these sprites of Venus were tugging at the stamens of a chime of fuchsias, like boys merrily pulling the ropes of wedding bells. Each piece differed from the others, but there was a love in every one. My wife was in raptures over the beautiful china, the exquisite elves, the graceful flowers, the delicate sentiments, the poetry in the artist's soul thus moulded into form—hardened into a thing of beauty, a joy forever. She could not restrain her exclamations of delight, as course succeeded course, even in the presence of the sedate attendants. Each new beauty called forth a new expression of wonder and pleasure. She would scarce allow anything on her plate, so anxious was she to study the devices and designs. I was calmer, being older, hungrier, less ethereal, and feeling an inner consciousness that a heavy bill would be the successor of these fairy scenes.

Even this dinner came to an end, long though we toyed over the dessert. The china afforded a ceaseless topic of conversation, until at length little fairies of another kind began to hang upon the long black lashes which veiled my wife's beautiful brown eyes, and we passed into our bed-chamber.

Over the mantel-piece of our dormitory hung a card, on which was printed the following:

"TAKE NOTICE.

"This building is fire-proof.

"Several robberies having taken place during the night, in the principal hotels, the proprietor respectfully requests all visitors to use the night-bolt.

"Money, jewelry, or articles of value are requested to be left at the bar, otherwise the proprietor will not hold himself responsible for any loss. "A. B., Proprietor."

My wife, who was rapidly increasing in legal, knowledge and acuteness under my able instructions, and was filled with the romantic idea of becoming a veritable helpmate to me in my profession as well as in the expenditure of my money, after reading the notice asked me if I was going to hand over my valuables. I told her that Pollock, C. B., had announced to the world that it was his opinion that such a notice did not apply to those articles of jewelry which a person usually carries with him—his watch, for instance—because, as the learned judge puts it, such an article would be of little service to the owner if it were nightly stowed away in the hotel safe.[1] His lordship, however, was inclined to think that if the watch were a richly jeweled one, set in valuable diam nds, it would be wiser to give it to the proprietor to keep."[2]

[1] Morgan v. Ravey, 6 Hurl. & N. 265.   [2] Ibid.

"But that is an English decision," remarked my wife, filled with the genuine occidental opinion of oriental notions.

"Well, supposing it is," I made answer, "it is in accord with the American; and a New York judge once said that although a watch, a gold pen, and pencil-case might in some sense be called jewels, still they should be considered part of a traveler's personal clothing, or apparel — and one after retiring to rest for the night is not expected to send down his ordinary clothing or apparel to be deposited in the safe."[1]

"But," continued Mrs. Lawyer, "this notice is not exactly the same as what one generally sees; it says nothing about the proprietor not being liable for the loss of things above a certain sum."

"No," I replied, "and it's all the better for us; for if the notice required by law is not properly posted up in the office and bedrooms, the proprietor cannot claim the benefit of the provision relieving him from the liability imposed upon him by the common law of making good all losses and damage to his guests' goods and property, unless caused by act of God, or of public enemies. It has been held in Iowa that such a notice as this one does not affect the landlord's position."[2]

"To what extent can he shirk his liability?" queried my wife, glancing at her large and well-filled Saratoga.

"That depends upon the particular statute of

[1] Giles v. Libby, 36 Barr. 70. But see Hyatt v. Taylor, 51 Barb. 632, and Rosenplanter v. Roessle, 54 N. Y. 262.
[2] Bodwell v. Bragg, 29 Iowa 232.

the country or State in which he happens to live.
If there is not a special law, no notice will bind the
guest, unless it can be proved that he has seen it
before he takes possession of his room,[1] or has
assented to it.[2]   In England, an innkeeper, if he
cause at least one copy of the law, (printed in plain
type,) to be exhibited in a conspicuous part of the
hall or entrance to his inn, will not be liable to
make good any loss of or injury to goods or property
brought to the inn, to a greater extent than £30,
(unless it be a horse or other animal, or any gear
appertaining thereto, or any carriage) except when
such goods have been stolen, lost, or injured,
through the willful act, default, or neglect of the
publican, or any servant in his employ; or when
such goods have been deposited expressly for safe-
keeping with mine host, who, in such case, may
require them to be placed in a box, or other recep-
tacle, fastened and sealed up by the guest.[3]   In
New York, the law is very similar,[4] being to the
effect that the hotel-keeper shall not be liable for
loss of money, jewels, ornaments, or valuables,
when he shall have provided a safe for the custody
of such property, and shall have posted a notice to
that effect in the room occupied by the guest, and
the guest shall have neglected to deposit such
property in the safe.[5]   So particular are the courts

---

[1] Morgan v. Ravey, 30 L. J. Ex. 131.

[2] Bernstein v. Sweeney, 33 N. Y. Sup. Ct. 271.

[3] Imp. Stat., 26 and 27 Vict., chap. 41, sec. 1. A similar
statute is in force in Ontario, only the money is limited to
forty dollars. (37 Vict. O., chap 11, secs. 1-4.

[4] Statutes of 1855, chap. 421.

[5] Wisconsin has a like law. (Laws of 1864, chap. 318.)

upon this point, that when the landlord of the Old
Ship Hotel, Brighton, England, unintentionally had
the notice misprinted, so that the little word *act*
was omitted in the sentence, which should have
been, (as I have just stated) 'where such property
shall have been stolen, lost, or injured through the
willful act, default, or neglect of such innkeeper,
or any servant in his employ,' the Court of Appeal
held that, as the notice contained no statement
which admitted the continuance of the common-
law liability for goods or property stolen, lost, or
injured through the willful act of the innkeeper or
his servant, the proprietor was not protected. But
Lord Cairns carefully said that he was not pre-
pared to hold that the omission, in good faith, of a
word or two, not material to the sense and to the
operation of the statute, would have such a disas-
trous effect." [1]

" My husband, remember

> 'Brevity's the soul of wit,
> And tediousness the limbs and outward flourishes,'

and be brief. How can my poor brain hold all that
you have said?"

" Don't be alarmed, my dear, there is doubtless
plenty of room in your brain yet. But I was going
on to say that though there is a tendency in these
degenerate days to lessen the great responsibility
once imposed upon these publicans and sinners, and
to insist upon greater care on the part of the
guests, still statutes limiting the common-law lia-

[1] Spice v. Bacon, L. R. 2 Ex. Div. 463; 16 A. L. J. 385.

bility of innkeepers should not be extended to include property not fairly within the terms of the acts. Where, for ·instance, as in the New York act, money, jewels, or ornaments are· exempted, then all property of a different kind, including all things useful and necessary for the comfort and convenience of the guest—all things usually carried and worn as part of the ordinary apparel and outfit, as well as all things ordinarily used or suitable to be used by travelers in doors or out, are left *in statu quo ante* the statute."

"And what may that be?" asked Mrs. L.

"At the risk of the innkeeper." 1

"But would not a watch be considered a jewel or an ornament?"

"The law is very watchful—"

"Very watchful, indeed, when it has so many watch cases that it considers pretty little Genevas neither jewels nor ornaments," murmured my wife *sotto voce*.

"The law is very watchful," I went on, "over benighted travelers, and has decided that it is. not; 2 nor is a watch and chain,3 although, by the way, the Wisconsin judges have decided that an innkeeper is not liable for the loss of a silver or a gold watch not handed over for safe keeping, their act speaking of articles of gold and silver manufacture.4

1 Remaly *v.* Leland, 43 N. Y. 538; Kellogg *v.* Sweeney, 1 Lans. N. Y. 397.

2 Remaly *v.* Leland, *supra*.

3 Bernstein *v.* Sweeney, 35 N. Y. 271; Krohn *v.* Sweeney, 2 Daly, N. Y. 200; Milford *v.* Wesley, 1 Wilson, (Ind.) 119.

4 Stewart *v.* Parsons, 24 Wis. 241.

The exemption is intended to apply only to such an amount of money and to such jewels and ornaments or valuables, as the landlord himself, if a prudent person and traveling, would put in a safe (if convenient) when retiring at night. No one, possessed of half a grain of that scarce commodity, common sense, would suppose that it was the intention of the act to exempt the hotel proprietors from their old common-law liability, unless the traveler emptied his pockets of every cent of money and deposited it, with his watch and pencil-case, in the safe, for perchance he might want these identical articles ere sweet sleep his eyelids closed.[1] If, however, the innkeeper has complied with the requirements of the act, he is not liable for jewelry stolen from the bedroom, even though the guest has not been guilty of negligence, provided he has had time and opportunity to make the deposit.[2] My old friend, Mrs. Rosenplanter, was terribly unfortunate in this respect. In July, 1863, she and her worthy spouse were *en route* from Trenton Falls to Saratoga, and arrived at the Delavan House, Albany, at three in the afternoon. As dinner was on the table, they at once dressed and went to dine. In about twenty minutes they returned to their room and found that in the meantime their trunk had been broken open and $300 worth of jewelry taken out. My friend sued the proprietor, but the court ungallantly considered that she had had sufficient time and opportunity to make the de-

---

[1] Giles *v.* Libbey, 36 Bar. 70.
[2] Rosenplanter *v.* Roessle, 54 N. Y. 262.

posit, (though she had not been there an hour) and
so could not recover; although the judge admitted
that no person, under such circumstances, would
have been likely to have handed over his valuables
to the innkeeper, and that there must always be a
brief period after the arrival of a guest before he
can make the deposit, and that during those golden
moments the statute affords the publican no protection. And, by the way, I remember that in this
case the court seemed to think that if a guest, on
retiring for the night, removes a watch or jewelry
from his person, or leaves money in his pocket, and
neglects to deposit the same in the safe, the hotel-
keeper, if he has complied with the act, is exempt
from all liability in case of loss." [1]

"You said," remarked Mrs. Lawyer, whom the
mysteries of the toilet had revived, "you said that
if the innkeeper put up his notice he would not be liable to make good any loss of goods or property. Surely, if a watch is neither an ornament nor a jewel,
within the meaning of the act,[2] it is goods or property, else it is not good for much."

"It is very questionable whether the words
'goods or property' include the necessary baggage
of a traveler, his watch or personal effects, or such
money as a man in his travels usually carries with
him; in fact, down South it was held that it did
not comprehend baggage." [3]

"Well, what would you call baggage?" per-

[1] Rosenplanter v. Roessle, 54 N. Y. 262; Bendetson v. French,
46 N. Y. distinguished.
[2] 11 Can. Law Jour. N. S. 103.
[3] Pope v. Hall, 14 La. An. 324.

sisted my wife. "It would be worth while knowing
that, if an innkeeper is always responsible therefor."

"Just wait until I comfortably settle myself, and
I will dilate on that fruitful topic until you are satisfied."

"What a base slanderer is Jules Verne," said my
spouse, as she daintily nestled between the sheets.

"What do you mean?" I asked.

"Don't you remember that he says that American
beds rival marble or granite tables for hardness. I
am sure he never stopped at a good hotel."

"Now for a Caudle lecture as to the baggage," 1
said. "*Imprimis*, whatever a traveler on this sub-
lunary planet takes with him for his own personal
care and convenience, or even for his instruction
and amusement,[1] according to the habits and wants
of the station of society to which he belongs, either
with reference to the immediate necessities or the
ultimate purpose of his wanderings, must be considered personal luggage; [2] and the rules of law
governing the innkeeper's liability for the safety of
a guest's baggage, are the same as those which reg-
ulate the responsibility of common carriers as to a
passenger's baggage.[3] Articles of jewelry, such as
you would usually wear, are baggage; [4] but not
the jewels and regalia of a society.[5] A watch,[6]

[1] Hawkins *v.* Hoffman, 6 Hill, 586.

[2] Macrow *v.* G. W. Rw. L. R. 6 Q. B. 622.

[3] Wilkins *v.* Earle, 18 Abb. N. Y. 190.

[4] Brooke *v.* Pickwick, 4 Bing. 218; McGill *v.* Rowand, 3
Penn. St. 451.

[5] Nevins *v.* Bay State S. B. Co. 4 Bosw. 589.

[6] Jones *v.* Voorhes, 10 Ohio, 145; Miss. C. Rw. *v.* Kennedy,
41 Miss. 471.

except in Tennessee;[1] finger-rings,[2] but not silver spoons,[3] come within the same category. One man was allowed to have two gold chains, two gold rings, a locket, and a silver pencil-case."[4]

"He must have been on his way to see his sweetheart, I fancy."

"Gold spectacles are baggage;[5] so are opera glasses,[6] a silver-mounted pistol, even for a Southern lady,[7] duelling pistols,[8] or a gun;[9] but not a colt."[10]

"A horse, then?" was facetiously queried.

"Not even a hobby-horse.[11] Brushes and razors, pens and ink, are baggage,[12] and perchance a present.[13] So are the manuscripts of a student;[14] but not the pencil sketches of an artist;[15] on this latter point, however, the doctors of the law disagree.[16] According to one judge, a concertina, a flute, or a fiddle might pass muster; but his fellows, however much music they had in themselves, determined

[1] Bonner v. Maxwell, 9 Humphrey, 621.
[2] McCormick v. Hudson River Rw. 4 E. D. Smith, 181.
[3] Giles v. Fauntleroy, 13 Md. 126.
[4] Brutz v. G. T. R. 32 U. C. Q. B. 66.
[5] Re H. M. Wright, Newberry Admiralty; Sasseen v. Clark, 37 Ga. 242.
[6] Toledo & Wabash Riv. v. Hammond, 33 Ind. 379.
[7] Sasseen v. Clark, 37 Ga. 242.
[8] Wood v. Devon, 13 Ill. 746.
[9] Davis v. C. & S. Rw. 10 How. Pr. 330.
[10] Giles v. Fauntleroy, 13 Md. 126.
[11] Hudston v. Midland Rw. L. R. 4 Q. B. 366.
[12] Hawkins v. Hoffman, 6 Hill, N. Y. Rep. 589.
[13] Gt. W. Rev. v. Shepherd, 8 Ex. 38. But see Bell v. Drew, 4 E. D. Smith, 59.
[14] Hopkins v. Westcott, 7 Am. Law. Reg. N. S. 533.
[15] Mytton v. Midland Rw. 4 H. & N. 615.
[16] Macrow v. Gt. W. Rw. L. R. 6 Q. B. 622, Cockburn, C. J

not to be moved with concord of sweet sounds, so
they out-voted their musical confrere.[1] Shake-
speare saith, 'Let no such man be trusted;' so, perchance, we must conclude that these judges were
astray in their law. In Pennsylvania, a journeyman
carpenter may take his tools as baggage,[2] though
in Ontario he cannot,[3] any more than a blacksmith
can carry his forge, or a farmer his plow. Nor can
a merchant take his wares,[4] nor a commercial his
samples,[5] nor a banker his money,[6] nor a lawyer his
papers,[7] though an M. D. may take his surgical instruments;[8] nor may a seamstress carry her sewing
machine,[9] nor—Hark!

"What strain is this that comes into the room,
At midnight, as if yonder gleaming light,
Which seems to wander like the moon,
Were seraph-freighted? Now it dies away
In a most far-off tremble, and is still;
Leaving a charmed silence.
Hark! one more dip of fingers in the wires!
One scarce-heard murmur struggling into sound,
And fading like a sunbeam from the ground,
Or gilded vanes of dimly visioned spires!"

Here a fantasia on her nasal organ (which my
wife always carried with her, despite the decisions

[1] Brutz v. G. T. Rw. 32 U. C. Q. B. 66.
[2] Porter v. Hildebrand, 14 Pa. St. 129.
[3] Brutz v. G. T. R. supra.
[4] Gilox v. Shepherd, 8 Ex. 30; Pardee v. Drew, 25 Wend.
459; Shaw v. G. T. Rw. 7 U. C. C. P. 493.
[5] Belfast B. L. & C. Rw. v. Keys, 9 Ho. Lords Cas. 556;
Hawkins v. Hoffman, 6 Hill, 586.
[6] Phelps v. London & N. W. Rw. 19 C. B. N. S. 321.
[7] Ibid.
[8] Giles v. Fauntleroy, 13 Md. 126.
[9] Brutz v. G. T. Rw. supra.

of anti-musical judges) vibrating unmistakably through the chamber, dispelled the idea of heavenly visitants, and informed me that my spouse had journeyed off to that land of Nod, from whose bourn no baggage returns. Snoring, like yawning, is infectious — sometimes; and this was one of the times.

* * * * *

" 'Tis sweet to see the day dawn creeping gradual thro' the sky," and feel that there is for one yet a little sleep, a little slumber, a little folding of the hands to sleep; but even in the most fashionable hotel the hour will at length come when one must shake off dull sloth and burst the bonds of sleep, which at night are but as spider's webs, but in the morning have become even fetters of brass; and that miserable hour came in time to me.

When I went down stairs to examine the register to see who had arrived during the night, I found some excitement existing around the office. On inquiry, (and who except a German savant ever beheld a row, small or great, without seeking to know the wherefore thereof,) I learned that a gent had the day before given the clerk a pocket-book to keep, and that it had been stolen out of the desk; the owner was demanding restitution, dollar for dollar and cent for cent, if not eye for eye and tooth for tooth. The landlord said that the man had been negligent in not telling the clerk there was money in the book.

"No, I wasn't," was the reply, "there was only $136 in it; and what but money would you expect.

to be in a pocket-book — a tooth-pick? — a cigar? I know that in Iowa an innkeeper had to cash up in a similar case,[1] and I'll make you do it if there is law or justice in this part of the American eagle's eyry."

"In Kentucky," said a by-stander, who seemed to hail from that State, "an hotel-keeper was held liable for the loss by robbery of pocket money retained by a guest in his own possession."[2]

"And in Maryland," said another Southerner, "it has been decided that a traveler need not deposit in the office safe any money reasonably necessary for his expenses that he may have with him."[3]

"Yes," I said, "there are other cases, also, which appear to establish the point that a sojourner at an hotel may keep in his pocket or in his room money enough to pay his daily way, and that if his purse be surreptitiously disposed of, the landlord must make good his loss;[4] yet still there is a very late New York decision, where my friend Hyatt found to his cost, that where a landlord provides a safe,' and puts up the usual notices about it, and the visitor chooses not to place his money in it, the proprietor of the establishment is not responsible for the loss of any of the cash, not even for what would

[1] Shoecraft v. Bailey, 25 Iowa, 553.
[2] Weiseinger v. Taylor, 1 Bush, 275.
[3] Maltby v. Chapman, 25 Md. 307 ; a decision under Md. Code, art. 70, secs. 5, 6.
[4] Taylor v. Monnot, 4 Duer, (N. Y.) 116; Van Wyck v. Howard, 12 How. (N. Y.) Pr. 147; Stanton v. Leland, 4 E. D. Smith, (N. Y.) 88; Simon v. Miller, 7 La. An. 360.

be required for the guest's ordinary traveling expenses." [1]

"You speak of money enough for one's daily wants and traveling expenses being all that for which an innkeeper is liable," said a gentleman who had hitherto been a quiet listener.

"Well, sir, I do not like to speak dogmatically, but it seems that the tendency of some modern decisions is to hold that the innkeeper should not be liable for any money beyond that amount, even though put in a safe, unless a special contract has been made, or it has been actually delivered to the proprietor or his servant, with notice not only of the kind of property it was, but also of the amount. It is not sufficient to mark a package 'money,' for it is argued that it would be highly unjust, and not founded upon any principle on which an innkeeper's liability rests, for a traveler to bring into an inn, unobserved, any amount of valuables, without notice to the innkeeper, and hold him responsible for their safe keeping. There should be a restriction or qualification of such liability, if it exists; and that must be a warning to the innkeeper of the extra risk he is about to run.[2] But the Court of Appeals in New York State takes a different view, and holds that if one complies with the law, and deposits his money in the safe, the innkeeper is liable for the full amount, irrespective of the question whether or not it was all required for the purposes of the journey.[3]

[1] Hyatt v. Taylor, 51 Barb. N. Y. 632; 42 N. Y. 259.
[2] Wilkins v. Earle, 18 Abb. N. Y. 190.
[3] Wilkins v. Earle, 44 N. Y. 172.

"And, I might add," said my interlocutor, "the
celebrated Story made no exception, and seemed to
consider it one of the A B C principles of law that
an innkeeper is liable for the loss of the money of
his guest, stolen from his room, as well as for his
goods and chattels, and that such liability extends
to all the money of the guest placed within the inn,
and is not confined to such sums only as are necessary and designed for ordinary traveling expenses.[1]
Then, sir, our great Chancellor Kent lays it down
as admitting of no peradventure, that an innkeeper
is bound absolutely to keep safe the property of his
guest within the inn, whether he knows of it or not,
and that his responsibility extends to all his guest's
servants, and to all the goods, chattels, and moneys
of the guest, their safe custody being part of the
contract to feed and lodge for a suitable reward.[2]
If you are not satisfied with the words of these men
—alike the pride and the ornament of America—
let us cross the ocean and hear what Sir Wm.
Blackstone saith; he speaketh after this wise: that
an innkeeper's negligence in suffering a robbery of
his guest is an implied consent to the robbery, and
he must make good the loss.[3]   Then Lord Tenterden held that there was no distinction between
money and goods; and all the other judges of the
court said 'amen.' "[4]

"Excuse my interrupting you in your interesting
remarks," said I.

1 Story's Commentaries, sec. 481.
2 Commentaries, sec. 470.
3 i Black. Com. 430.
4 Kent v. Shuckard, 2 B. & Ad. 803.

"Quite excusable, sir, for I am only speaking in the cause of right, and because I think some judges are inclined to cut loose from the safe moorings of the old common law, rendered dear to us by the adjudications of the learned men of the Bench for generations past, both in the old and new worlds; and I am satisfied that a contrary doctrine will be terrible in its effects in this great commercial community of ours, where our business men spend so large a portion of their time at inns in pursuit of their calling.[1]   But what were you going to say?"

"Simply," I remarked, "that in the case before Tenterden the amount lost was only £50, and it was stated to have been kept to meet daily expenses only.   He said he could see no distinction in this respect between an innkeeper and a carrier; and there are many cases to the effect that a carrier will not be responsible for any money of a passenger except what is needful for traveling purposes and personal use,[2] unless the loss was occasioned by the gross negligence of the carrier."

"Well, other English judges have likewise held that an innkeeper's liability is not restricted merely to the guests' travelling expenses;[3] and if we recross the mighty ocean we find our judges in firm accord with their confreres."[4]

---

[1] Per McCann, J., Wilkins v. Earle.

[2] Orange Co. Bank v. Brown, 9 Wend. 85; Weed v. Saratoga & Sch. Rw. 19 Wend. 524; Red. on Railways, vol. 2, pp. 55, 58.

[3] Coggs v. Barnard, 1 Sm. Leading Cases, 309; Lane v. Cotton, 12 Mod. 487; Wharton on Innkeepers, 97.

[4] Cole v. Goodwin, 19 Wend.

"But," I said, "but in one case the amount was only two hundred dollars,[1] and in another it was but twenty-five dollars.[2]   And in still another case decided, as you say, although the cash lost was more than sufficient to pay the expenses of the man from whom it was taken, still it was not his own; he merely held it to pay others, who were stopping at the same house, and were witnesses in a suit which the money-holder was superintending, or to pay their expenses at the inn."[3]

"On the other hand," said the defender of the rights of the people, "in a California hotel there was this notice: 'Deposit your valuables and money in the safe at the office;' and a guest accordingly deposited a large amount of gold dust and coin, which the proprietor received without objection.   Afterwards, the clerk was knocked down and the safe robbed, it not being locked, and the publican was held liable for the whole amount.[4] And where a man had stolen from his room a package of jewelry, which the clerk had told him would be quite safe there, the host was held liable, even in New York State.[5]   And so, in Kentucky, where a safe was robbed by a discharged clerk, although in this last case the innkeeper had told the guest that he would not be responsible for any money put in it.[6]   It seems to me to be somewhat absurd that

[1] Quintin v. Courtney, Hay. (N. C.) 41.
[2] Giles v. Libby, 36 Barb. 70.
[3] Berkshire Woollen Co. v. Proctor, 7 Cush. 417.
[4] Pinkerton v. Woodward, 33 Cal. 557.
[5] Bendeton v. French, 44 Barb. 31.
[6] Woodward v. Bird, 4 Bush. (Ky.) 510.

the law should say that unless you deposit your money in the hotel safe the proprietor will not be liable for its loss, and then when you have placed it in the absolute and immediate control of the inn-keeper, and, perhaps, his dishonest servant, you should be met the next day, when asking for your own, by the smirking and bowing proprietor, re-marking, *suaviter in modo:* 'True, sir you gave me twenty thousand dollars for safe-keeping, and I put it in my safe; but, like all riches, it has taken to itself wings and flown away. However, my dear sir, here are one hundred dollars to pay your expen-ses, and take you comfortably to your journey's end.'"

"There appears to be something to be said on both sides," I remarked, wearying of the discussion from which all others, save my adversary and my-self, had long since fled; for when the time comes for my funeral expenses to be incurred, no one will be able (whatever my readers may think) to say of me, as they did of Lord Macaulay,

'There was no pain like silence, no constraint
So dull as unanimity. He breathed
An atmosphere of argument, nor shrunk
From making, where he could not find, excuse
For controversial fight.'"

"But I have the best of it," said my antagonist. "It is a case of New York State, like Athanasius, *contra mundum.*"

"At all events, you will agree with me that an innkeeper will not be liable for loss of his guest's money when he has intrusted it to the care of some

one else on the premises in whom he reposes confi-
dence,"[1] I replied.

"Certainly; and I remember a case where a man
gave a bag of money to the step-daughter of an
innkeeper with whom he was particularly intimate,
having courted her in marriage, and the bag having
disappeared, the owner thereof got nothing.[2] And
I trust that you will not deny that the innkeeper is
responsible, notwithstanding any notices up about
depositing in the safe, if the guest has not had time
to get his valuables put in there after his arrival."[3]

"Oh, yes; and he is liable for their loss after the
visitor has taken them out preparatory to his departure."[4]

Here two bows were exchanged, two backs
turned, and four legs walked off.

[1] Houser v. Tulley, 62 Pa. St. 92.
[2] Sneider v. Geiss, 1 Yeates, 24.
[3] Rosenplanter v. Roessle, 54 N. Y. 262; Bendetson v. French,
46 N. Y.
[4] Stanton v. Leland, 4 E. D. Smith, 88.

Chapter VI.

FIRE, RATS, AND BURGLARS.

After a time, business called me in the direction in which the "tide of empire rolls," and we took a long, but by no means tedious or monotonous journey, along that metal ribbon which, stretching from ocean to ocean, unites the Atlantic to the Pacific. The train was well supplied with saloon cars, balcony cars, restaurants, smoking cars, palace cars, and sleeping cars. We encountered none of the adventures so graphically described by the writer of the veracious history of Phineas Fogg; no herd of ten thousand buffaloes delayed, no daring band of Sioux attacked, our train; we had neither duel nor flying leap over bridges, crashing down into abysmal depths. We ate, we drank, we slept, we talked, we gazed; we gazed, we talked, we slept, we drank, we ate; and that was all.

At last we reached the wondrous " City of the West," and beheld the mighty waters of the Pacific throbbing upon the shores and along the piers of San Francisco. To the Palace Hotel we drove, and there we took up our quarters, glad enough to rest our brains, dizzied and dazed with our flight across the continent.

Refreshed by the quiet rest and needful repose of a long night's sleep, my wife insisted upon taking a stroll through the magnificent hotel in which we were now quartered.

"If there was a railway running along all the passages and corridors we might manage to get round the Palace Hotel in a morning," I said, "but steam has not yet been introduced for that purpose. To be sure, there is the pneumatic tube, but that is not quite large enough unless you are willing to go without a pannier."

"How large is the house?" asked Mrs. Lawyer.

"Why, it is three hundred and fifty feet long by two hundred and seventy-five broad."

"Let us hurry, then ; if it is so huge we have no time to lose," was the brave response.

"Well, here's an elevator," I remarked.

We stepped into one of the four passenger elevators, which are run by hydraulic power.. The motion was almost imperceptible, and rapid as the downward flight of a swallow. The young gent in charge told us that it could run from bottom to top and back again to bottom, through the whole seven stories of the house, in ten seconds.

On arriving on the ground floor we first inspected the grand court and the rooms on either side, and then turned into one of the long corridors, from which my wife insisted upon visiting the handsome stores, opening off with their tempting wares. I left her making purchases while I entered the barber's saloon, and in one of the easiest of patent adjustible chairs, by the deftest of tonsors, with the keenest of razors, allowed myself to be shaved; for Mrs. L. loved not to see a man with his nose projecting over a cascade of hair, and desired that my face might preserve its human outline, instead of presenting—as she sarcastically remarked—no distinction from the physiognomy of a bearded owl or a Barbary ape.

No fear of losing nose or cheek while in that place. But, after all, it is not a sublime attitude for a man to sit, with lathered chin, thrown backward, and have his nose made a handle of. To be shaved, however, is the fashion of American respectability, and it is astonishing how gravely men look at each other when they are all in the fashion. For the benefit of those unfortunates who get gashed betimes beneath the operator's hand, I would say, that if a barber attempts to shave you he must possess the necessary education and skill, and show the diligence of an expert in that line, otherwise he will be liable for damages sustained.[1] Of course if you suffer an inexperienced volunteer to practice upon your chin and you come to grief, you have no remedy, unless the amateur is guilty of gross negligence; but if one unskilled in the art pushes himself forward and seizes you by the nasal projection, to the exclusion of a professional, he is expected to use the skill usually possessed by a master of the art.[2] In Illinois, it would seem that if one renders his services free, gratis, and for nothing, he will be only liable for gross negligence;[3] but the point appears open to argument.[4] I presume that no one would be so foolish as to suppose that a professor of the tonsorial art is bound to

[1] Wharton on Negligence, secs. 50, 730.
[2] Wharton on Neg. sec. 732; Hood v. Grimes, 13 B. Mon. 188.
[3] Ritchey v. West, 23 Ill. 385.
[4] Wharton on Negligence, secs. 437, 641.

attend to your hirsute appendages willy-nilly; but when he does take you in hand he must carry the operation through without any sins of omission or commission.[1]

When I rejoined my wife, she asked to descend into the basement regions, so down we went, and found bath-rooms and laundry-rooms, wine-rooms, pantries, etc., in well nigh endless succession.

"How many napkins do you use a day?" inquired Mrs. L. of the individual whose duty it was to reside in a region of perpetual steam and damp.

"About three thousand," was the response; "and four hundred table-cloths, if people are reasonably careful."

"I would like some things washed; how soon could you do them?" asked my wife.

"If they are large articles, you can have them back in your room in fifteen minutes; if small, in seven minutes."

"That's rather quick," I remarked.

"Well, sir, I have known a man to have his shirt washed while taking a bath; and a handkerchief, sent down the tube dirty, was returned clean during the time he was arranging his neck-tie, or parting his back hair."

On we went, to the pantries, and saw the thousands and tens of thousands of pieces of china and crockery, glass and cutlery.

"A breakage occasionally would not matter much, among so many thousands of pieces," I remarked.

[1] Wharton on Negligence, sec. 731.

"It would matter more to the man who broke the article than to the hotel proprietor, I calculate," responded the man in charge of this legion of crockery and glassware.

"Well, sir, that depends on how the breakage occurred. I take it that a guest at an hotel is, with respect to the things that he uses, in the same position as if he hired them—in fact he does hire them; and it is well settled that every hirer of a chattel is bound to use the thing let to him in a proper and reasonable manner, to take the same care of it that a prudent and cautious man ordinarily takes of his own property, and to return it to the owner at the proper time, in as good condition as it was in when he got it, subject only to deterioration produced by ordinary wear and tear, and reasonable use, and injuries caused by accidents which have happened without any default or neglect on the part of the hirer.[1] The owner must stand to all the ordinary risks to which the chattel is naturally liable, but not to the risks occasioned by negligence or want of ordinary care on the part of the hirer.[2] In fact, as a late writer has very well put it, the hirer of a chattel is in no sense an insurer, nor is he liable for *culpa levissima*, or that apocryphal phrase of infinitesimal negligence which stands in antithesis to the *diligentia diligentissima* which the law does not, as a continuous service, exact."[3]

[1] Jones on Bailments, 88.
[2] Addison on Contracts, 415.
[3] Wharton on Negligence, sec. 713.

As I paused, the man hastily remarked that he had no time to stop and talk, and my wife, fearing that the subterranean air was affecting my brain, said that we had better go up stairs; so, like the youth with the strange device, "Excelsior" was our motto.

"Take that box of matches," said Mrs. Lawyer. "We may want them when off picnicking."

"We had better not. They are left there for the purpose of lighting cigars, and can only be taken in a limited manner. Taking them by the boxful would be larceny, if the intent is felonious,"[1] I returned.

"What a terrible place for a fire!" suggested my wife.

"Yes," I replied. "No fire would have the slightest chance here. What with the huge reservoir supplied by artesian wells, the seven tanks on the roof, the three large steam fire-pumps, the watchmen going their constant rounds, and the thermostats in every room in the hotel, (which, when the temperature is raised to 120°, cause a bell to be rung continuously in the office, and show the number of the room affected in the annunciator) a spark could scarce develop itself into a blaze before its discovery."

"Well, but," urged Mrs. Sawyer, "suppose, notwithstanding these precautions, a fire did take place, and our baggage was destroyed, would the landlord have to pay for it?"

"I can only say, my dear, that on the other side

[1] Mitchum *v.* The State, 45 Ala. 29.

of the continent, in the State of Vermont, where a man sued to recover the value of a span of horses, a set of double harness, two horse-blankets, and two halters, it was decided by the court that an hotel-keeper is not liable for property lost by fire where the conflagration is occasioned by unavoidable casualty or superior force, without any negligence on his part or that of his servants.[1] An English decision tends in the same direction;[2] and in Michigan it was held that he was not liable for the horses and wagons of a guest, burned in a barn, without his negligence.[3] But the English decision has been questioned both here and there,[4] and in New York it was considered that the liability of a publican extended to the loss of goods by fire, (though the cause of it was unknown) provided that the guest is free from all blame in the matter.[5] In that State they have a law exempting landlords from liability for the loss by fire of a guest's goods in a barn or outhouse, if it is shown that the damage is the work of an incendiary, and occurred without negligence on their part; but the burden of proving this is, of course, upon the innkeeper,[6] and my own humble opinion is that an innkeeper is liable for all such losses unless they are caused by a public enemy, or an act of God, (lightning,

---

[1] Merrill v. Claghorn, 23 Vt. 177; also Vance v. Throckmorton, 5 Bush. (Ky.) 41.

[2] Dawson v. Chamney, 5 Q. B. (N. S.) 164.

[3] Cutler v. Bonney, 30 Mich. 259.

[4] Mateer v. Brown, 1 Cal. 225; Wharton on Neg. p. 111.

[5] Hulett v. Swift, 33 N. Y. 571.

[6] Faucett v. Nicholls, 64 N. Y. 377.

or an earthquake) or the owner has been negligent."[1]

*   *   *   *   *

· "Heigh–ho!" sighed my wife, as, exhausted with her long tramp through the mammoth house, she sank into a luxurious arm-chair on our return to our own apartment, preparatory to an excursion through the city. "Look at that horrid little thing!" she exclaimed the next instant, and starting up with enough vehemence to frighten a lion, she scared away a little mouse that had been nibbling at her reticule. "The little wretch! see how it has spoilt my nice new satchel! It must have been the cakes inside. Can I make the landlord give me a new one?" she avariciously added.

"Humph! I wish that some one had asked me that question who could afford to pay me for a carefully considered opinion," I replied.

"Why can't you tell me?"

"Because I scarcely know what to say. The point seems open to argument. I don't remember any case where the depredations of mice have occupied the attention of a court of law, although there have been several decisions on the subject of rats."

"Well, and what were they?" exclaimed my wife, impatiently. "That a man can keep the nasty things in his house, and let them damage the property of his guests, and not pay for them?"

"In one case where rats gnawed a hole in the bottom of a boat, and the water, coming in at the

leak, damaged goods on board, the owner of the
vessel was held liable for the performance of those
rodents;[1] and in another case, carriers were held
responsible for their depredations on board a ship,
although there were cats and mangooses on board,
and the owners had availed themselves of the valuable services of the venerable sire of the pretty
rat-catcher's daughter of Paddington Green."[2]

"But you stupid man, we are not on board ship,"
said my amiable and accomplished spouse.

"And," I replied, "that is exactly where the
difficulty arises; for where a man had a water-tank
on the roof of his house, and the rats gnawed
through a leaden pipe so that water trickled down
and injured the goods of another fellow on the
ground floor, the court held that the owner of the
establishment, who occupied the upper flat, was not
responsible—and Chief Baron Kelly remarked that
it was absurd to suppose that a duty lay on the
landlord to exclude the possibility of the entrance
of rats from without."[3]

"That seems a very different view from that
taken by the judges in the other cases," remarked
Mrs. L.

"Yes; but the Chief Baron said that the case of
a ship was wholly different—that it might be possible to insure freedom from rats in a ship, but that
it was impossible to say that this could be done
with respect to warehouses generally,[4] and another

[1] Dale v. Hall, 1 Wils. 281.
[2] Kay v. Wheeler, L. R. 2 C. P. 302.
[3] Carstairs v. Taylor, Law R. 6 Ex. 217.
[4] Carstairs v. Taylor, *supra*.

judge remarked that a landlord could not be considered negligent if he omitted taking means to get
rid of these pests till there was reason to suppose
they were in the building."[1]

"Never mind what others considered and thought
and said—what do you think?"

"I think that perhaps the rule would apply that
if a man permits an animal to remain in his possession he becomes liable for the mischief it com-
mits."[2]

"Do you know what I think?" queried my wife.

"No, my dear."

"That we had better go to lunch."

*   *   *   *   *   *

As we were quietly sleeping the sleep of the wearied just that night, I was aroused by a noise at our
window. In a moment or two it was opened, and
then a man stealthily entered the room. I had not
time to ask him what he wanted, for at the first
sound of my voice he was off as quickly as if he
had heard the click of a pistol. I made the window secure, and again entered dream-land. In the
morning, as we donned the attire which Adam's
transgression has rendered necessary, my wife and
myself conversed on the subject of the liability of
an hotel-keeper for losses occurring to his guests
from burglary.

"In Vermont, my dear," I said, "it has been held
that if the proprietor could show that the burglari-
ous entry was under circumstances that absolved

[1] Ibid. per Bramwell, J.
[2] McKome v. Word, 5 Car. & P. 1.

him from all blame, he would not be liable.[1] But that doctrine is not now followed." [2]

" And what do the judges now say? "

" It was decided in this sunset State that although the point may be somewhat unsettled, yet still the true idea is to hold that innkeepers, like common carriers, are insurers of the property committed to their charge, and are bound to make restitution for any injury or loss not caused by the act of the Almighty, nor by a common enemy, nor by the neglect or default of the owner."[3]

A fresh topic of conversation here suggesting itself to the active brain of Mrs. L., she launched out upon it *con amore.*

I found afterwards that I had not been the only object of the burglar's attentions, for as I was sauntering along one of the corridors of the hotel I was accosted thus:

" I say, you walking digest of the law of inns and innkeepers, what's the consequence if a guest is a little careless and loses his valuables? "

This question was familiarly put to me (that is, put in a way that evinced no intention on the part of the speaker of paying for the information sought) by an old friend, with whom I occasionally conversed on legal topics, and from whom carelessness and negligence were as inseparable as Apollo and

[1] McDaniels *v.* Robinson, 26 Vt. 311; Morse *v.* Shee, 1 Vent. 190, 238.

[2] Mateer *v.* Brown, 1 Cal. 221; Norcross *v.* Norcross, 53 Me. 163; Pinkerton *v.* Woodward, 33 Cal 557.

[3] Mateer *v.* Brown, *supra.* See, also, Mason *v.* Thompson, 9 Pick. 284.

his golden bow, or Orpheus and his tuneful lyre.

"The same old Story, to whom I have often alluded in my professional talks with you, says [1] that negligence may be ordinary, or less than ordinary, or more than ordinary; and that ordinary negligence may be defined to be want of ordinary diligence, and gross negligence to be want of slight diligence. Although some English judges have said that they can see no difference between negligence and gross negligence; that it is the same thing with the addition of a vituperative epithet.[2] Of what kind of negligence have you been guilty, and what has happened?"

"I did not say that I had been doing anything. But suppose that a fellow had some money in his portmanteau and left it in the hall of the hotel with the other baggage, and didn't say anything about it to the landlord, and it disappeared."

"Well, sir, in such a case I should say that a jury would be warranted in finding that the individual referred to had been guilty of gross negligence, and that the hotel-keeper was exonerated through his imprudence in thus exposing his goods to peril."[3]

"I had some such idea floating through my own cranium."

"'Tis a pity that your brain is in such a liquid state. I remember a case of a man of the name of Armistead, a commercial traveler, who, while at an

[1] Story on Bailments, sec. 17.
[2] Rolfe, B. in Wilson v. Brett, 11 M. & W. 110; Austin v. Manchester &c. Railway, 10 C. B. 474.
[3] Fowler v. Dorlon, 24 Barb. 384.

hotel, placed his box in the commercial room, as was the wont of those who visited the house. The box had money in it, and was left there for three nights. Twice or thrice, in the presence of several on-lookers, Armistead opened the trunk and counted his change. The lock was so bad that any one could unfasten it without a key by simply pushing back the bolt. The money leaked away mysteriously, and Armistead sued the landlord to recover it, but the judge who tried the case told the jury that gross negligence on the part of the guest would relieve the host from his common-law liability; and when the matter came up before the court it was held that the jury had done right in finding the traveler had been guilty of such gross negligence as to excuse his landlord from liability for the money. Lord Campbell remarked that the judge would have been astray had he said that in all cases a box should be taken to the guest's bedroom, and he doubted whether, in order to absolve the innkeeper, there must be *crassa negligentia* on the part of the guest." [1]

"That's the law, is it?"

"A still more recent case settled the question as to the amount of negligence that would bind the owner of the goods. In deciding it, Earle, J., said that he thought that the rule of law resulting from all the authorities was, that in a case like the one he was considering the goods always remained under the charge of the innkeeper and the protection of the inn, so as to make the landlord liable as for

[1] Armistead *v.* White, 29 Law J. Q. B. 524.

10.

breach of duty, unless the negligence of the guest
occasions the loss, in such a way as that it would
not have happened if the guest had used the ordinary care that a prudent man might reasonably
have been expected to take under the circumstances;[1] and the same rule seems to hold good on this
side of the Atlantic."[2]

"If a friend bags your baggage," inquired the
searcher after cheap knowledge, "at an hotel, and
marches off with it, could you compel the proprietor of the establishment to make good your loss?"

"It was decided not, in Illinois, where one had
allowed his chum to exercise acts of ownership over
his trunk;[3] and long ago it was held, in the old
land, that if a landlord tells a guest, on his arrival,
that he has no room, the house being full, and his
words are veritable truth, and yet the guest insists
upon being admitted, saying that he will shift for
himself, or if he go and share the apartment of
another, without the consent of the proprietor or
his servants, the host is not responsible for his
traps, unless the sufferer can show that the goods
were actually stolen or lost through the negligence
of the innkeeper or his servants.[4] But an innkeeper can't shirk his liability because his house is
full of parcels, if the owner is stopping at the
house."[5]

---

[1] Cashill v. Wright, 6 El. & B. 898.
[2] Chamberlain v. Masterson, 26 Ala. 371; Hadley v. Upshaw,
27 Tex. 547; Profiles v. Hall, 11 La. An. 324.
[3] Kelsey v. Berry, 42 Ill. 469; Cayle's Case, 8 Coke, 32.
[4] 1 Andess. 29.
[5] Bennett v. Mellor, 5 T. R. 273.

"To tell you, then, what really did happen to me: I got in here late last night, and after entering my name at the office, pulled out my purse and paid the cabby; I then went to my room, and being very tired, tumbled out of my clothes as rapidly as nature and art would permit me, put them on a chair near the bed, and was soon among the flowery meads of dream-land. This morning, lo and behold! the purse which I had left in my pocket was gone, some villain having, while I slept, entered the room by the door, which I had omitted to fasten. Now, then, what are my rights and remedies in the premises?" asked my friend.

"In the days when the Virgin Queen, Elizabeth, ruled the benighted land of our ancestors, and trifled with the affections of subject, prince, king, czar, and Cæsar, the whole Court of Queen's Bench decided that an innkeeper was bound by law to keep the goods and chattels of his guests, without any stealing or purloining, and that it was no excuse for him to say that he delivered to the guest the key of his bed-room, and that he (the guest) had left the door open, (that is, I presume, unlocked);[1] for that he, the landlord, is responsible for their safety, even in the bed-room, and that even though the poor publican never knew that his visitor had any property with him, and was entirely ignorant of the depredation. Unless, indeed, the thief was the guest's servant or friend, or the proprietor had required the guest to place his goods in a particular chamber, under lock and key, saying that then he

---

[1] Erle, J., in Cashill v. Wright, 6 El. & B. 895.

would warrant their safety, otherwise not, and the
man had foolishly neglected the advice."[1]

"Ah, well! then I am all right."

"Kindly refrain from forming a definite opinion
until you are in full possession of the whole law on
the subject. I know that it has been held again
and again, in England, that a guest is not bound to
either fasten or lock his door.[2] In a very late case
Lord Chancellor Cairns remarked that he would be
sorry to say any single word implying that there is
any rule of law as to this;[3] and our own authorities seem to be in unison with the English decisions.[4] But perhaps you may have heard the remark that circumstances alter cases."

"I must confess the maxim has a ring not altogether novel to my ears."

"I may say that it is particularly true in legal
matters; and sometimes it is incumbent on a guest
to fasten his door.[5] For example, a commercial
traveler obtained a private room wherein to exhibit
his goods to his customers. Clements, the landlord,
told him to lock the door. This the man neglected
to do, although while showing his samples a stranger
had twice popped his phiz into the room. The court
considered that the traveler by his own act had absolved Clements from his liability, and that he must
bear his loss as philosophically as possible."[6]

[1] Cayle's Case, 8 Coke, 32.
[2] Mitchell v. Woods, 16 L. T. Rep. N. S. 676; Filipourke v.
Merryweather, 2 Fost. & F. 285.
[3] Spice v. Bacon, 16 Alb. L. J. 386.
[4] Classen v. Leopold, 2 Sweeney, (N. Y.) 705.
[5] Baddenberg v. Benner, 1 Hilt. (N. Y.) 84.
[6] Burgess v. Clements, 4 Moore & S. 306.

FIRE, RATS, AND BURGLARS.

"Did the occupants of the bench state the why and the wherefore?"

"Yes; and it was partly on the ground that the hotel-keeper was not bound to extend the same protection to goods placed in a room for the purposes of trade as to those in an ordinary chamber. (You know the liability is only as to baggage; it extends not to merchandise.)[1] And further, that circumstances of suspicion had arisen which should have put the guest on his guard; that after the vision of the strange head it became his duty, in whatever room he might be, to use at least ordinary diligence, and particularly so as he was occupying the apartment for a special purpose. For though, in general, a traveler who resorts to an inn may rest upon the protection which the law casts around him, yet, if circumstances of suspicion arise, he must exercise at least ordinary care."[2]

"But," said my companion, "I had no head to warn me—not even Banquo-like did any 'horrible shadow, unreal mockery' appear, to place me on my guard."

"A case occurred at Bristol, in England, which may, perchance, put the matter to you in a clear light. A man of foreign extraction, Oppenheim by name, went to the White Lion Hotel. While in a public room he took from his pocket a canvas bag, containing twenty-two gold sovereigns, some silver, and a £5 note, and extracted therefrom a tanner —"

[1] Pettigrew v. Barnum, 11 Md. 434; Giles v. Fauntleroy, 13 Md. 126.

[2] Burgess v. Clements, *supra*.

" A what ? "

" A six-penny bit—to pay for some stamps. Shortly afterwards he retired for the night to a room in an upper story; the door had both lock and bolt; the window looked on to a balcony. The chambermaid told him that the window was open, but said nothing about the door. He closed the latter, but did not lock it or bolt it; left the window open, and placed his clothes, with the money in a pocket, on a chair at his bedside. During the night some one entered by the door and removed the bag without first removing the money from it. Of course Oppenheim sued the hotel company, and had the pleasure of hearing the judge tell the jury that they should consider whether the loss would or would not have happened if O. had used the ordinary care which a prudent man might reasonably be expected to have used under the circumstances."

" And the jury said what ? "

" Why, they said the hotel company were not liable; and the Court of Common Pleas, at Westminister, said that the judge had put the law correctly, and that the jury had done their duty."

" But then the guest had been guilty of other acts of negligence besides leaving his door unlocked; he showed his purse— "

" *Et tu Brute!* " I remarked.

" I forgot," was the confession.

" The whole facts of the case must be looked at; and the judges thought there was evidence of negligence on Oppenheim's part which contributed to the loss. One of my Lords said that he agreed in the opinion that there is no obligation on a guest at an inn to lock his bedroom door; but the fact of the guest having the means of securing himself and choosing not to use them is one which, with the other circumstances of the case, should be left to the jury. The weight of it must, of course, depend upon the state of society at the time and place; what would be prudent at a small hotel in a small town might be the extreme of imprudence at a large hotel in a city like Bristol, where probably three hundred bedrooms were occupied by people of all sorts.[1] And one of the other judges remarked that Lord Coke, in the case to which I first referred,[2] only meant that an hotel-keeper could not get rid of his liability by merely handing his guest a key, and that he by no means laid it down that a guest might not be guilty of negligence in abstaining from using it."[3]

"Well, what am I to do?"

"Do! Why let the past bury the past, and in future remember three golden rules whenever you are at an hotel. First, under any circumstances lock your bedroom door when you retire for the night. Secondly, do not display your cash in public places; and, Thirdly, consider whether there are not special circumstances calling for special caution on your part, and if there are, act accordingly. But you have not told me yet how much you lost."

[1] Per Montague Smith, J.; Oppenheim v. White Lion Hotel Co. L. R. 6 C. P. 515.

[2] Cayle's Case.

[3] Oppenheim v. White Lion Hotel Co. *ante.*

"Only $2; but it is the principle involved that I look at."

"You rascal! if I had known that it was such a paltry sum, I would not have taken the trouble to tell you all that I have."

CHAPTER VII.

HORSES AND STABLES.

Time passed, and back to the East we had come. On a certain day my wife and myself, together with a couple of friends, yclept Mr. and Mrs. De Gex, engaged a carriage and pair to take us some twenty or thirty miles into the country to see some wonderful sights—what they were is quite immaterial at this late date. A pleasant drive and charming day we had. The night we were to spend at a little village inn.

The mistress of the small establishment received us right warmly, so that a perfect glow of pleasure pervaded one's inner man.

"Ah," said Mrs. De Gex, who was inclined towards sentimentalism, "how true are the words of the poet!

'Whoe'er has traveled life's dull round,
    Where'er his stages may have been,
May sigh to think that he has found
    His warmest welcome at an inn.'"

The innkeeper told our driver to leave the carriage outside on the road. One of the party asked if that would be safe.

"If it is not," I replied, "Boniface is responsible, for I remember that, in England, a man drove up to an inn on a fair day and asked the landlord if he had room for the horse, and a servant of the establishment put it into the stable, while the traveler took his coat and whip into the house, where he got some refreshment. The hostler placed the gig in the open street, (outside the inn-yard) where he was accustomed to leave the carriages of guests. The gig having been stolen, the publican was held liable." [1]

"That seems rather hard, when, perhaps, the yard was full," some one remarked.

"The landlord was not bound to receive the gig if he had not sufficient accommodation for it. The guest did not know whether there was room or not; and as the hostler took the horse, he had a right to assume that there was. If the proprietor had wished to protect himself he should have told the traveler that he had no room in the yard, and that he would have to put the gig in the street, where, however, he would not be liable for it. He did not do so, and had to bear the penalty.[2] And it has been held in this country that an innkeeper would be responsible in the same way where a guest's servant had placed his master's property in an open, uninclosed space, by the direction of the hostler, and upon being assured that it would be quite safe there." [3]

"Mr. Justice Story once said that in the country towns of America it is very common to leave chaises and carriages at inns under open sheds all night, and also to leave stable doors open and unlocked; and that if, under those circumstances,

---

[1] Jones v. Tyler, 1 Ad. & E. 522.
[2] Taunton, J., in Jones v. Tyler.
[3] Piper v Manny, 21 Wend. 283.

a horse or a chaise should be stolen, it would deserve consideration how far the innkeeper would be liable,"[1] said Mr. De Gex, my companion, who had looked inside a law-book or two.

"I fancy it has been considered," I replied, "and the innkeeper has met with little consideration, and is held bound to protect the property of those whom he receives as his guests. In one instance, the driver put his loaded sleigh in the wagon-house of the inn, where such things were usually placed; and the doors of the shed having been broken open and property stolen, the landlord was held bound to make good the loss, without loss of time.[2] But Dr. Theophilus Parsons, who knows something of these matters, says that if a horse or carriage is put in an open shed with the owner's consent or by his direction, the innkeeper will not be liable for their loss, and that where this is usually done and the owner of the horse knows the custom and gives no particular instructions, it may be presumed that he consented and took the risk upon himself."[3]

"Suppose we inspect the stable and see what accommodation there is for our equine friends." We entered. "Rather risky place to put two city horses in," De Gex continued. "Look at the flooring. A nag of any spirit, not accustomed to the place, might kick through it and break its leg."

"Well," I said, "the innkeeper is bound to provide safe stabling for the horses of his guest, and if any evil betide the animals from being improp-

[1] Story on Bailments, sec. 478.
[2] Chute r. Wiggins, 14 Johnson, 175.
[3] Parsons on Contracts, vol. 2, p. 169.

erly tied, or the stalls being in bad repair, full
compensation may be recovered.[1] He is responsible from the moment he receives the quadrupeds
until they leave; even after the owner has paid his
bill and his man is harnessing them to go;[2] and,
as a rule, the statutory laws limiting the liability of
hotel-keepers do not apply to horses or carriages."

"Your view is the one a lawyer (a man without
a heart) might take of it, but a merciful man is
merciful to his beast and does not like to run the
chance of its being killed."

"The tavern-keeper's liability extends even to
the death of the animals in his care,"[3] I remarked.

"Still, one should himself exercise reasonable
care and caution," returned De Gex. "I remember
a gentleman, who kept his horse at an inn, rode
out one evening and on returning himself took it
into the stable and tied it up in the stall in which
it had usually been kept. The next morning the
horse was found dead in the same stall, its head
wedged fast in the trough, which was made of a
hollow beech log having a bulge in the middle,
thus rendering that part wider than the top. The
poor beast had evidently killed itself in trying to
extricate its head. The owner brought an action
against the publican, but had to bear the loss, not
only of his horse but also of the suit."[4]

"Yet I know that where a horse had been choked

---

[1] Dickenson v. Rodgers, 4 Humph. (Tenn.) 179.

[2] Seymour v. Cook, 53 Barb. 451.

[3] Metcalf v. Hess, 14 Ill. 129 ; Hill v. Owen, 5 Blackf. (Ind.)
323.

[4] Thickstern v. Howard, 8 Blackf. 535.

to death by its halter, and it was proved that it was tied under the superintendence and direction of the owner himself, and in reply the owner proved that the stall in which it had been was in very bad condition, it was held that the innkeeper could not give further evidence.[1] And when another innkeeper agreed with the owner of a horse to entertain the man in charge one day in every week, or oftener if he should chance to stop at the inn with the horse, furnish the latter with provender and allow it to be kept in a particular stall: no one but the man in charge took care of the horse; yet on its being injured in its stall, the innkeeper was held answerable."[2]

"And look, besides, there are no proper partitions between the stalls," said my friend, "and some other nag might kick one of ours; and you know that it was decided in the old country that under such circumstances the publican would not be liable for the injuries so inflicted, unless it could be proved that he did not take due and proper care in excluding vicious and kicking horses."[3]

"Hah!" I exclaimed. "But that case has since been doubted, and it can scarcely be accepted as good law.[4] Well, what shall we do?"

"Let's tell them to turn the nags into the field," said De Gex.

"If you do, and they are lost, stolen or injured,

[1] Jordan v. Boone, 5 Rich. 528.
[2] Washburn v. Jones, 14 Barb. 193.
[3] Dawson v. Chamney, 52 B. 33.
[4] Wharton on Innkeepers, p. 111; Matier v. Brown, 1 Cal. 221.

we cannot look to our host for recompense, unless Master Boniface himself be guilty of negligence, as by putting them in a field where pits or ditches abound or fences and gates are broken or open. If, however, he should put them into the pasture of his own accord, he would be answerable;[1] for then the field would be considered as part of the inn premises. Although Story thinks that the latter rule should be qualified, as it is such a common custom in America in the summer time to put horses in a pasture, he says the implied consent of the guest may fairly be presumed, if he knows the practice."[2]

"Well, let us send them over to the other house, where the stabling appears better, while we ourselves lodge here," again suggested Mr. De G.

"That might do," I made answer; "for an innkeeper is bound to receive a horse, even though the owner chooses to go elsewhere.[3] And it is clearly settled that in the eyes of the law a man becomes a guest at a place of public entertainment by having his horse there, though he himself neither lodges nor takes refreshments there."[4]

"But I thought that an innkeeper was not bound to take the goods of a man who merely wishes to use the house as a place of deposit;[5] nor liable for things so left there, except as an ordinary bailee."[6]

[1] Cayle's Case, 8 Rep. 32; Hawley v. Smith, 25 Wend. 642.

[2] Story on Bailments, sec. 478.

[3] Saunders v. Plummer, Orl. Bridg. 227.

[4] Mason v. Thompson, 9 Pickering, 280.

[5] Bennet v. Mellor, 5 T. R. 273.

[6] Wintermute v. Clarke, 5 Sandf. 242; Smith v. Dearlove, 6 C. B. 132.

"Oh, that rule only applies to dead things out of which the man can make no profit; but with animals the innkeeper is chargeable, because he makes something out of keeping them. And, as I said, it has been frequently held that he is liable for the loss of a horse, although its owner puts up at a different place. But there is some doubt."[1]

"Will he also be liable for the carriage?" asked my companion.

"Yes, and for the harness as well; for the compensation paid for the horses will extend the host's responsibility to such articles. And the owner will be able to sue for damages if anything happens to our nags, although they have been hired by us.[2] If a servant brings his master's horse to an inn, and while there it is stolen, of course the master can sue the innkeeper;[3] and for all such legal purposes the hirer of goods will be deemed the owner's servant."

"Suppose a horse-thief stops at an inn and there loses his prize, can the owner then sue the land-lord?"

"No; he must, under those trying circumstances, look simply to the person who first deprived him of his faithful nag,"[4] I replied.

"The other innkeeper may charge pretty well for the horses, if we stay here ourselves," suggested De Gex.

---

[1] Peel *v.* McGraw, 25 Wendell, 653; York *v.* Grindstone, 1 Salk. 388; Sturt *v.* Dromgold, 3 Bulst. 289. But see Grinnell *v.* Cook, 3 Hills, N. Y. 686; Ingallsbee *v.* Wood, 33 N. Y. 577; 36 Barb. N. Y. 425; Nowers *v.* Fethers, 61 N. Y. 34; Healey *v.* Gray, 68 Me. 489.

[2] Mason *v.* Thompson, *supra.*

[3] Bacon's Abr. Inns and Innkeepers, C.

[4] Bacon, *supra.*

" In the good old days of yore he could not have done that, for innkeepers were bound to ask only a reasonable price, to be calculated according to the rates of the adjoining market, without getting anything for litter;[1] and if they made a gross overcharge, the guests had only to tender a reasonable sum, and have them indicted and fined for extortion.[2] But I fear me those halcyon days have passed. Do you know that if a man is beaten at an inn the proprietor is not answerable, although if the man's horse should be so treated, even if it were not known who did it, the publican will be liable?"[3]

" That is queer law. Why is it?"

" Because in ages long since gone by an innkeeper's liability was confined to one's *bona et catalla*, and injury to a man is not damage to his *bona et catalla*."

" Well, I am sure I don't see what would damage his ' bones and cartilage,' if a good beating did not. Let us join the ladies."

" I think we had better, after that atrocious attempt at a pun," I replied. " Well said the Autocrat of the Breakfast Table, ' a pun is *prima facie* an insult to the person you are talking with. It implies utter indifference to, or sublime contempt for, his remarks, no matter how serious.' "

We found our better halves had gone out for a walk. Knowing that their feminine curiosity would soon bring them to a standstill we started in pursuit, and speedily came up with them as they stood

[1] 21 Jac. I, chap. 21, sec. 2.
[2] 1 Hawk. 225.
[3] Cayle's Case, 8 Rep. 32; Stammin v. Davis, 1 Salk. 404.

gazing at some rose bushes in a pretty flower garden.

"Did you ever see such bea-u-ti-ful roses?" screamed Mrs. De Gex, whose voice, when pitched in a high key, was as melodious as a peacock's.

"And so many!" added Mrs. Lawyer.

"I am somewhat a believer in the doctrine of metempsychosis," said Mr. De Gex.

"What has such a horrid thing to do with roses?" asked his wife.

"Merely that, if it be true, I may have seen finer and more numerous flowers long, long ago."

"Explain," I exclaimed.

"Well, when in another form I may, at the beginning of the Christian era, have been present at the regatta near lovely Baiæ and seen the whole surface of the Lucrine Sea strewn with these flowers, according to custom; or I may have been present at some of old Nero's banquetings, when he caused showers of rose-leaves to be rained down upon the assembled guests; or, in fact, I may have been at Heliogabalus' dinner party, when such heaps of these same flowers were flung over the revelers that several were smothered to death. That frail beauty, Cleopatra, was wont to spend immense sums on roses, and at one entertainment, that she gave in honor of her friend Anthony, she had the whole floor covered more than a yard deep."

"How delightful!" chorused the ladies.

"The Sybarites used to sleep upon beds stuffed with rose-leaves. That old tyrant Dionysius, at

his revels, constantly reclined on a couch made of
the blossoms. Verres, with whom Cicero had the
tussle, was accustomed to travel through his prov-
ince reclining gracefully on a mattrass full of them;
and not content with this, he had a wreath of roses
round his head and another around his neck, with
leaves intertwined. And Antiochus, when he
wanted to be uncommonly luxurious, would sleep
in a tent of gold and silver upon a bed of these
flowers."

"Did they indulge in attar?"

"I cannot say, but at his parties, Nero—that
champion fiddler of Rome—would have his foun-
tains flinging up rose-water; and while the jets
were pouring out the fragrant liquid, white rose-
leaves were on the ground, in the cushions on
which the guests lay, hanging in garlands on their
noble brows, and in wreaths around their necks.
The *couleur de rose* pervaded the dinner itself, and
a rose pudding challenged the appetites of the
guests, while, to assist digestion, they indulged in
rose wine. Heliogabalus was so fond of this wine
that he used to bathe in it."

"What a waste!" said my wife.

"Whose? That girl's?" I asked.

"You horrid man!" returned my wife. "But I
know you pretend to dislike roses."

"Yes," I said, "if metempsychosis is correct, I
must have been killed two or three times during
the Wars of the Roses. I believe, with the ancient
Aztecs, that sin and sorrow came into the world
through the first woman plucking a forbidden
rose."

"He is, perhaps, not quite so bad as the lady who had such a strong antipathy to this queen of flowers that she actually fainted when her lover approached her wearing an artificial one in his button-hole; nor as good Queen Bess's lady-in-waiting, who disliked the flower so much that her cheek actually blistered when a white one was placed upon it as she slept. He is most like Tostig of old," continued my wife.

> " He cannot smell a rose but pricks his nose
> Against the thorn and rails against the rose."

Our position changed and so did the subject.

* * * * *

The next day when we went over for our horses we found a most interesting discussion going on between the landlord and a man of a class somewhat too common in these hard times, an impecunious lawyer, concerning the right of the former to detain the horse of the latter for the hotel bill of the owner.

"You can't do it," said the poverty-stricken disciple of Coke. "No innkeeper can detain the other goods and chattels of a guest for payment of the expenses of a horse, nor a horse for the expenses of the guest. You can only keep my horse for the price of its own meat, and that has been paid for.[1] If a man brought several horses to your old inn, each one could be detained only for its own keep, and not for that of the others; and if you let the

[1] Rosse v. Bramstead, 2 Rol. Rep. 438; Bac. Abr. vol. 4, p. 411; Parsons on Contracts, vol. 3, p. 250. But see Mulliner v. Florence, L. R. 3 Q. B. D. 454.

owner take away all but one, you could not keep
that one until your whole bill was paid, but you
would have to give it up on tender of the amount
due for its keep.[1] Hullo!" he added, as he saw me,
"here's a gentleman who knows all about such things.
Is not what I state correct?" he coolly asked.

"Certainly," I said, turning. to the landlord.
"Mr. Blackstone's law is better than his pay;
though, perhaps, Mr. Story may be said to doubt
his last statement."[2]

"But," said Boniface, a short, fat man, made
without any apparent neck at all—only head and
shoulders like a codfish—"but the rascal did not
pay me for the last time he put up his old beast
here, and I'll keep it now till I am paid or till it
dies, which latter event will probably happen first to
such a bag of bones."

"You can't do that, old boy," said Mr. B., de-
lightedly.

"He is right again," I replied. "If you let a guest
take away his horse, unless, indeed, he merely takes
it out for exercise, day by day, *animo revertendi*,[3]
it amounts to giving him credit and a relinquish-
ment of your right of lien, so that you can't afterwards retake it. And even if the man was to come
back and run up another account for the keep of
his horse, although you might detain it for the latter debt, you could not for the former."[4]

---

[1] Moss *v.* Townsend, 1 Bulstr. 207. But see Story on Bailments, sec. 476.

[2] Story on Bailments, sec. 476.

[3] Allan *v.* Smith, 12 C. B., N. S. 638.

[4] Jones *v.* Thurloe, 8 Mod. 172; Jones *v.* Pearle, 1 Strange.
556; Parsons on Contracts, vol. 3, p. 250.

"But have I no lien upon the horse of a guest? Besides, I did not let him take it away. He went off with it at daybreak, before any one was up, the villain," said mine host, waxing more and more wrathy as the thought of past grievances recurred to him.

"He, he, he!" laughed B. "You might have retaken it if you had been spry enough, and then you might have kept it; but now it's too late, too late, too late, as the song says."[1]

"Exactly so," I added. "Of course, my dear sir, there is little doubt but what you have a right to detain a horse, brought to you by a traveler, for its keep.[2] And if you kept that old nag you would have a perfect right to continue to charge for the food supplied from day to day, while it remained in your possession, and that although Mr. B. distinctly told you that he would not be responsible for anything supplied to his horse; because otherwise your security would soon be reduced to the value of an old hide and bones.[3] But then *cui bono?*"

"What's that?" asked the astonished innkeeper.

"I mean, what would you gain by the additional outlay of good fodder?" I explained.

"Why, I would make the old thing work!" replied the man.

"No, indeed!" said Blackstone. "You would

[1] Ross *v.* Bramstead, 2 Rol. Rep. 438.
[2] York *v.* Grindstone, 2 Ld. Raym. 866. But see Fox *v.* McGregor, 11 Barb. (N. Y.) 41; Saint *v.* Smith, 1 Caldw. (Tenn.) 51.
[3] Gilbert *v.* Berkeley, Skin. 648. And see Scarfe *v.* Morgan, 4 M. & W. 270; and Somes *v.* B. Emp. Ell. Bl. & Ell. 353.

have no right to ride on my horse, or use him for your own benefit in any way." [1]

"You would have no more right to use it for your own pleasure and benefit than a man who distrains a cow for rent has to enjoy the fruits of her ruminations. You could only ride the horse for the purpose of preserving its health by proper exercise," [2] I remarked.

"I am dashed if I'd do that," cried the publican, waxing fierce.

"You would have to do it," [3] shrieked Blackstone, triumphantly.

"Well," then roared the master of the establishment, "I'd sell the blamed thing quick enough."

"If you did you would get yourself into hot water, and have to pay me the full value of the beast; for an innkeeper can't sell a horse he detains for its board without the consent of the owner. [4] Ho! ho! ho!" laughed the little rascal.

The poor landlord looked at me with such a despairing glance—a look of a dying duck in a thunder-storm—that I could scarce restrain my risible faculties as I remarked:

"I am afraid your adversary is correct, and not even if a horse were to eat its head off could you sell it, unless you chanced to live in London or

[1] Westbrooke v. Griffith, Moor. 876; Jones v. Thurloe, 8 Mod. 172; Mulliner v. Florence, L. R. 3 Q. B. D. 489.

[2] Westbrooke v. Griffith, supra.

[3] Idem.

[4] Jones v. Pearle, Str. 556; Thames I. W. Co. v. Pat. Derrick Co. 1 Johns. & W. 97; 27 L. J. C. 714; Mulliner v. Florence, L. R. 3 Q. B. D. 484.

Exeter. Your only remedy would be to sue for the price of the food, get judgment, and then sell.[1] You cannot sell a right of lien, or transfer the property, without losing your right and rendering yourself liable to an action. One must proceed by suit."[2]

The landlord turned to the rascally attorney, and shaking his fist at him, exclaimed: "Get out, and if ever you darken my door again—look out!"

"Keep cool, sir, keep cool, the day is warm. Don't shake your fist in my face, sir. It is not the first time I've done the old chap," added my unworthy confrere, turning to us with a look of importance; "and it will not be the last, unless I've read law for naught."

"How did you take him in before?" I queried.

"Well, some years ago I was hard up—not the first, perhaps not the last time I have been in that state—and I knew not how to get my team fed for a week or two. So, believing that money had a considerable influence with our friend here, I got a chap to run off with my ponies, bring them here, and throw out some hints that it would be all right in a pecuniary point of view if they could be kept in the stable for a few days until the affair blew over. All went merry as a marriage bell. I advertised for horses lost, stolen, or strayed, and after some three weeks happened here and quite accidentally, you know, found my span. Of course mine host wanted pretty good pay, but I talked to

---

[1] Wharton on Innk. 122; Cross on Lien, 345 *n.*

[2] Fox *v.* McGregor, 4 Barb. 41; Hickman *v.* Thomas, 16 Ala. 666; Miller *v.* Marston, 85 Me. 153.

him like a father; told him that I knew that if a
traveler brings to an inn the horse of a third person, the innkeeper has a perfect right to detain it
for its keep; that of course he was not bound to
inquire whose horse it was;[1] that that highly estimable and worthy occupant of the bench in days
that are no more, I mean Judge Coleridge, said
that with reference to an innkeeper's lien there was
no difference between the goods of a guest and
those of a third person brought by a guest.[2] This
pleased the old rascal. Then I pleaded poverty, but
Shylock was unmoved; then I assumed an appearance of anger at his keeping my horses and went
away."

"But how did that help you?" I asked impatiently, growing weary of a story that was long
enough for the ears of an antediluvian patriarch.

"Oh, I had not left the worthy's house five minutes before I happened, quite accidentally, you
know, to meet the man who had taken the horses.
Back we came. Boniface admitted that he was
the one who had brought my ponies to the inn.
Then said I: 'Sir, this man has confessed that he
told you that he did not own the horses, that he
had stolen them; you, therefore, became a party to
his crime and have no right to keep my horses any
longer for their charges. See—here is the law;' and
I showed him Oliphant on Horses, page 129;[3] and

---

[1] York v. Grenaugh, 2 Ld. Raym. 866; Robinson v. Walker,
Pop. 127.
[2] Turrill v. Crawley, 13 Ad. & E. (N. S.) 197; Manning v.
Hollenbeck. 27 Wis. 202.
[3] See, also, Johnson v. Hill, 3 Stark. 172.

the fellow at once caved in. Ta-ta, Mr. Law-yer."

And so off went the man to practice his knaveries and trickeries on some other unfortunate members of the *genus homo.* The only consolation of a virtuous man is that

> "Doubtless the pleasure is as great
> Of being cheated as to cheat."

" Well," said my friend, who had all this· time been standing by, a silent but not an unbenefited listener, " Well, it strikes me that the law concerning innkeepers and horses needs what Lord Dundreary thought the country did, that is to say, namely, to wit, improving!"

" True for you," I replied. " For instance, until recently it was doubtful whether an innkeeper who detains a horse as a pledge for its keep, can detain also the saddle and bridle, or even the halter which fastens it to the stall.[1] And where a man stopped with his horse at an inn under suspicious circumstances, and the police ordered the innkeeper to retain the animal, it was held that the poor landlord had no lien.[2] And if a neighbor leaves his nag with an innkeeper to be fed and kept, allowing him to use it at his pleasure, and a creditor of the owner seize it for a debt, the poor publican has no lien for the animal's keep;[3] nor would he have, where he

---

[1] Wharton, p. 120; Stirt *v.* Drungold, 3 Bulst. 289. But see Mulliner *v.* Florence, L. R. 3 Q. B. D. 484.

[2] Burns *v.* Pigot, 9 C. & P. 208.

[3] Grinnell *v.* Cook, 3 Hill, (N. Y.) 486.

boards the horses of a stage line, under a special agreement."[1]

"What about a livery-stable keeper?" asked De Gex.

"Down in Georgia, it was held that he had a right of lien on horses and buggies left in his keeping;[2] but everywhere else, it is considered that he has no such lien, for the contract with him is that the owner is to have the horse whenever required;[3] and the claim of a lien would be inconsistent with the necessary enjoyment of the property."[4]

"Suppose the livery man pays out money to a vet. for advice?"

"That would make no difference.[5]   But if a man who is both an innkeeper and a livery-stable keeper receives a horse, and does not say he takes it in the latter capacity, he has all the responsibilities of an innkeeper, as well as all his privileges.[6] On the other hand, if an innkeeper receives horses and carriages on livery, the fact that the owner on a subsequent day takes refreshment at the inn will not give the innkeeper an innkeeper's rights.[7] I was almost forgetting to say that even a livery-stable keeper may have a lien by express agree-

[1] Dixon v. Dalby, 9 U. C. Q. B. 79.

[2] Grammell v. Schley, 41 Ga. 112.

[3] Judson v. Etheridge, 1 C. & M. 743; Anderson v. Bell, 2 C. & M. 304; Parsons on Contracts, vol. 3, p. 250.

[4] Kinlock v. Craig, 3 L. R. 119; Taylor v. Robinson, 8 Taunt. 648; Jackson v. Cummins, 5 M. & W. 342.

[5] Orchard v. Rackstraw, 9 C. B. 698; Hickman v. Thomas, 16 Ala. 666; Thickstein v. Howard, 8 Blackf. 535.

[6] Mason v. Thompson, 9 Pick. 280

[7] Smith v. Dearlove, 6 C. B. 132.

ment;[1] and if he exercises any labor or trouble in the improvement of the animals, he will have a lien for his charges.[2]

" Well, I rather fancy that the ladies will think we have not almost, but altogether, forgotten them, and intend to pass another night here. Let us be off."

[1] Wallace *v.* Woodgate, 1 Ryan & M. 193.
[2] Jacobs *v.* Latour, 2 M. & P. 20; 5 Bing. 130; Jackson *v.* Cummins, 5 M. & W. 342; Harris *v.* Woodruff, 124 Mass. 205.

Chapter VIII.

WHAT IS A LIEN?

As we turned to leave the premises to hasten back to our respective wives, leaving our Jehu to bring the carriage and horses, we were accosted by a most dilapidated specimen of the genus "seedy," who appeared to be a kind of stable-boy or hostler not overstocked with brains. Judging from a cursory glance, his pants had parted in irreconcilable anger from his boots, and had cautiously shrunk well up to the knees—as if apprehensive of a kick from the big toe which was well enough to be outside the remains of the boots; here and there patches of bare skin peeped out through his tattered set-upons, as if pleased to see daylight and have a little fresh air. Yet of such varied hues were they, that the most profound ethnologist would be perplexed to decide whether the man should be classed among the Caucasian, Mongolian, Malay, Indian, or Negro race, or whether he was a hybrid compound of all five. His coat, in colors, would have rivaled Joseph's, and made the teeth of his naughty brethren water with tenfold jealousy. His hat might have for generations been used in winter to exclude the rains and snows from a broken window, in summer for the breeding place of barn-door fowls. The countenance of this tatterdemalion seemed as empty as his pockets, and his brain as disordered as his long yellow hair; his breath as alcoholic as the store-room of a distillery; his *tout ensemble* anything but suggestive of the "is he not a man and a brother" sentiment.

In piteous tones this wreck of what, perchance, was once a mother's darling, a father's pride, asked:

"Be you a liyur, sur?"

"Yes. What do you want?" I returned.

"Well, sur, I'm a poor man, with not a cint to bliss myself wid; and I come here one day and got a bite of vittals, and bedad, sur, the ould landlord seized me for rint, and said, says he, that he had a lane upon me for those same scraps of cold food; and says he, I must stay here and work for him until I can pay up. Now, kin he do that same, yur honor?"

"No, most certainly not. He has no right to keep you or any other man for such a reason.[1] So you had better be off."

"Long life to your honor, and may the holy saints—but kin he," and again the voice sank into a wail, "kin he kape me clothes?"

"Nothing that you have on,"[2] I replied, as I turned away, thinking that I could hear the scratch of the recording angel's pen as he scored another to the number of my good deeds.

"Was it not considered at one time that an innkeeper had the right to detain the persons of his guests for the payment of their bills?" queried De Gex.

---

[1] Sunbolf *v.* Alford, 3 M. & W. 254; Parsons on Contracts, vol. 3, p. 250.
[2] Ibid.

"Yes, old Bacon so lays it down,[1] and so did one Judge Eyres,[2] long since gone to his account; and in some of the old text-books the same view is taken. But the idea was exploded forty years ago by the combined effort of Lord Abinger, C. B., and his *puisnés*, Barons Parke, Bolland, and Gurney."

"On what occasion?"

"A man of the name of Sunbolf sued an innkeeper for assaulting and beating him, shaking and pulling him about, stripping and pulling off his coat, carrying it away and converting it to his own use."

"That was rather rough of him."

"It was, but the innkeeper, Alford, replied that he kept a common inn for the reception, lodging and entertainment of travelers and others; and that just before the time when he did all those things complained of, Sunbolf and divers other persons in company with him came into the inn as guests; and that he then found and provided them, at their request, with divers quantities of tea and other victuals; and that Sunbolf and the other persons thereupon, and just before the committing of the grievances, became and were indebted to him in a certain small sum of money, to wit, eleven shillings and three pence, for the said tea and victuals ; and thereupon he, the innkeeper, just before he did the things of which he was accused, required and demanded of Sunbolf and the others, payment by them, or some or one of them, of the said sum,

---

[1] Bacon's Abr. Inns. D.
[2] Newton *v.* Trigg, 1 Shower, 269.

or some security or pledge for the payment thereof; but Sunbolf and the others wholly refused
then, or at any other time, to pay to him the said
sum, or leave with or give to him any security or
pledge for the payment of the same; and before
he did the acts spoken of, Sunbolf persisted in
leaving, and would have departed and left the said
inn, against the innkeeper's will and consent, without paying the said sum of eleven shillings and
three pence, so due as aforesaid, had not he, A.,
kept and detained him, Sunbolf, or some other of
the said persons, or their goods and chattels, or
some of them, until they paid it; and because
Sunbolf and the others would go and depart from
the said inn without paying, and refused to pay
that sum to him, and because the sum remained
wholly due to him, and because Sunbolf and the
others would not, and refused to leave with or give
any pledge or security whatever to him for the
payment of that sum, and he (that is, Alford) could
not procure or obtain from them, or any or either
of them, any other pledge or security than the said
coat mentioned, he, (the said Alford) at the time
mentioned, did gently lay his hands on Sunbolf to
prevent him going and departing from the said inn
without his or the other persons paying the said
eleven shillings and three pence, or giving him
some pledge or security for the payment of it; and
he did then, for the purpose of acquiring such security or pledge, to a gentle and necessary degree,
lay his hands upon Sunbolf, and strip and pull the
said coat from and off of him, the same being a

reasonable pledge or security in that behalf, and then placed the same in the said inn wherein he had thence thitherto kept and detained the same as such pledge and security, for the said debt of eleven shillings and three pence, being wholly due and unpaid to him; and, therefore, he (Alford) suffered and permitted Sunbolf and the others to go and depart from the said inn; and on the occasion aforesaid he necessarily and unavoidably, to a small degree, shook and pulled about Sunbolf; and these were the acts complained of."

"Well said the wise man of old, '*Audi alteram partem*,'" said my friend. "Alford's story gives quite a different aspect to the whole affair."

"It gives you, at any rate, an idea of the long-winded pleadings in vogue in the year of grace 1838."

"Was A.'s explanation satisfactory to the court?"

"Oh, dear, no! Parke, B., asked, during the argument, if an innkeeper had a right to turn his guest out without a coat; or if he had a right to take off all his clothes, and send him away naked; and afterwards, in giving judgment, he clearly and distinctly answered his own queries, and said that an innkeeper had no power to strip a guest of his clothes; for if he had, then, if the innkeeper took the coat off his back, and that proved an insufficient pledge, he might go on and strip him naked, and that would apply either to a male or female——"

"That would be shocking!"

"The learned baron merely considered it utterly absurd, and that the idea could not be entertained

for a moment. Another of the judges said that he
had always understood the law to be that the
clothes on the person of a man, and in his possession at the time, are not to be considered as goods
to which the right of lien can properly apply ; that
the consequence of holding otherwise might be to
subject parties to disgrace and duress in order to
compel them to pay a trifling debt which, after all,
was not due, and which the innkeeper had no pre-
tence for demanding."

" But, my dear fellow, we were speaking of the
right of a landlord to keep the body of his guest."

" To be sure we were. The Chief Baron said
that if an innkeeper had a right to detain a guest for
the non-payment of his bill, he had a right to detain him until the bill was paid, which might be for
years or might be for aye ; so that by the common
law, a man who owed a small debt, for which he
could not be imprisoned by legal process, might
yet be detained by an innkeeper for life. Such a
proposition my Lord Chief Baron said was mon-
strous, and, according to my lord Baron Parke,
was startling." [1]

" For my part, I think it is high time we rejoined
the ladies," said De Gex, with the air of a man satisfied with what he had heard.

" All right; throw law to the dogs, to improve
upon the immortal bard."

*　　*　　*　　*　　*　　*

Our return drive was as pleasant as that of the

[1] Sunbolf v. Alford, 3 Mees. & W. 248.

preceding day, except that we might well have exclaimed, in the words of the poet:

> "How the dashed dry dust,
> Nebulous nothing,
> Nettled our nasal
> Nostrils, you noodles!"

En route, we stopped at a little wayside inn for luncheon: On the table the *pièce de resistance* was beefsteak.

"I never," observed De G., "see beefsteak but I think of poor old George III."

"Had he a particular *penchant* for it?" I asked.

"Not that. But once, when his intellect was sadly clouded, he was breakfasting at Kew, and the conversation turned on the great scarcity of beef in England. 'Why don't the people plant more beef?' asked his majesty. Of course he was told that beef could not be raised from seed or slips; but he seemed incredulous, and, taking some pieces of steak, he went out into the garden and planted them. Next morning he visited the spot to see if the beef had sprouted, and finding some snails crawling about, he took them for small oxen, and joyfully exclaimed to his wife: 'Here they are; here they are, Charlotte—horns and all!'"

"Poor fellow—poor fellow!"

By and by, apple dumplings appeared. "Ha!" I exclaimed, "here are more reminders of the poor old king! How his Britannic majesty used to puzzle over the problem of how the apples got inside the pastry."

"The Chinese cooks would have bewildered him still more with some of their ingenious performances," remarked De Gex.

"In what respect?" queried the ladies.

"At a recent banquet in San Francisco, an orange was placed beside the plate of each guest. The fruit, to an ordinary observer, appeared like any other oranges ; but, on being cut open, they were found to contain, *mirabile dictu*——"

"What?" asked my wife.

"Excuse me, I should not have quoted Latin. They were found to contain five different kinds of delicate jellies. Of course, every one was puzzled, first of all, to find how the jelly got in; and giving up that as a conundrum too difficult to be solved, he found himself in a worse quandary over the problem as to how the pulpy part of the orange got out. Colored eggs were served up, and inside of them were found nuts, jellies, meats, and confectionery."

"Wonderful men those Celestials!" I exclaimed. "They must have got such notions from the banqueting table of Jove himself."

"I thought they indulged in nothing nicer than cats or dogs, rats or mice, with an occasional dash of bird's-nest soup," said Mrs. De Gex.

"Altogether a mistaken notion," returned her husband.

Tea was the beverage. I nearly upset the table as I reached over for the teapot, whereupon my comrade exclaimed in the words of Cibber's rhapsody :

"Tea, thou soft, thou sober, sage and venerable liquid; thou female tongue-running, smile-smoothing, heart-opening, wink-tipping cordial, to whose glorious insipidity we owe the happiest moments of our lives, let me fall prostrate."

"Time's up," I said, as straightening myself I swallowed another cupful.

*   *   *   *   *

When we were again fairly under way and the ladies were quietly talking some scandal, *sotto voce*, I said to De Gex: "Referring again to the innkeeper's lien——"

"Let us have no more about it," he replied promptly. "Honestly, I must say that you are not a Paganini and cannot please by always playing upon one string."

"Perhaps not, but as rare old Ben Jonson remarked, 'when I take the humor of a thing once, I am like a tailor's needle—I go through,' and a little more information on that important subject may prove useful to you some day."

"If you will talk on that dry subject, kindly inform me why publicans have a lien at all," said my friend.

"Well, you know that a lien is the right of a man to whom any chattel is given to detain it until some pecuniary demand upon or in respect of it has been satisfied by the owner, and as the law treats an innkeeper as a public servant, and imposes upon him certain duties—making him, for example, receive all guests who are willing and able to pay, and are unobjectionable on moral, pecuniary, or hygienic grounds, and bestow on the preservation of their goods an extraordinary amount of care — so, to compensate him for this obligation, the law gives him the power of detaining his guest's goods, (except such as are in the visitor's actual possession and custody, in his hand for example,) until he pays for the entertainment afforded, including, of course, remuneration for the care of those goods. The lien extends to all the goods and chattels of the guest, even those especially handed over to the host and placed by him apart from the personal goods of his visitor."[1]

" Then, I suppose an innkeeper has a lien upon the goods of a guest only."

" Exactly so ; so that if he receive the person as a friend, or a boarder,[2] or under any special agreement,[3] or an arrangement to pay at a future time,[4] he has no lien upon the goods, for he has no responsibility with regard to them. In one case, however, it was decided that if a man came to an hotel as a guest, his subsequently arranging to board by the week would not alter the character in which he was originally received, nor take away the host's right of lien."[5]

" Suppose things are brought which the innkeeper is not bound to receive—what then?"

---

[1] Mulliner v. Florence, L. R. 3 Q. B. D. 485.
[2] Drope v. Thaire, Latch, 127; Grinstone v. Innkeeper, Hetl. 49 ; Pollock v. Landis, 36 Iowa, 651 ; Hursh v. Byers, 29 Mo. 469 ; Ewart v. Stark, 8 Rich. (S. C.) 423.
[3] Wintermute v. Clarke, 5 Sandf. 242.
[4] Wharton, p. 123.
[5] Berkshire Co. v. Proctor, 7 Cush. 417.

13.

"Where he actually takes in goods for a guest, whether he were legally bound to do so or not, he is responsible for their safety, and so has a lien upon them.[1]   But if anything is left with him, merely to take care of, by one who does not himself put up at the house, the poor innkeeper has no right to keep them until paid for his trouble;[2] unless, indeed, it is a horse, or other animal, out of the keep of which he can receive a benefit.[3]   And you heard old Blackstone say, this A. M., that the proprietor is not bound to inquire whether or not the guest is the real owner of the goods;[4] and if the guest turns out a thief, still the true owner cannot get back his property without paying the charges upon it.[5]   In Georgia, however, it has been held that the innkeeper has no lien against the true owner, except for the charges upon the specific article on which the lien is claimed."[6]

"But supposing he really knows that the guest is not the owner?" said my companion.

"Then he has no lien.   Broadwood, the celebrated piano manufacturer, loaned a piano to M. Hababier, who was staying at a hotel.   The court held that, as it was furnished to the guest for his temporary use by a third party and the innkeeper

[1] Trelfall v. Borwick, 41 Law J. Q. B. 266; affirmed, L. R. 10 Q. B. (Exch.) 210.

[2] Bennett v. Mellor, 5 T. R. 273.

[3] Allen v. Smith, 12 Com. B. N. S. 638 ; Peet v. McGraw, 25 Wend. 654.

[4] Johnson v. Hill, 3 Stark. 172 ; Kent v. Shuckard, 2 Barn. & Adol. 805.

[5] Johnson v. Hill, *supra.*

[6] Domestic Sewing Machine Co. v. Walters, 50 Ga. 573.

knew it belonged to such party, and as Hababier had not brought it to the place as his own, either upon his coming to or while staying at the inn, the proprietor had no lien upon it.[1] But of course, if a servant, or an agent, in the course of his employment, come to an inn and runs up a bill, the proprietor has a lien upon his master's goods in the servant's custody."[2]

"How long does this right last?"

"Only so long as the goods remain in the inn. If the guest goes away and then comes back again, the publican cannot retain them for the prior debt.[3] If, however, the unsophisticated landlord is beguiled into letting them go by a fraudulent representation, his right remains;[4] and if they are taken away, he may follow them if he does not loiter.[5] Delays are always dangerous, except in cases of matrimony. Of course, a tender of the money claimed extinguishes the lien;[6] but it must be a valid tender. Tossing down a lot of money on a table, and offering it if the innkeeper will take it in full of the bill, is not a proper tender.[7] Sometimes, if too much is claimed, or the claim is on a wrong account, a tender may not be necessary."[8]

[1] Broadwood v. Granara, 10 Ex. 423. See, also, Carlisle v. Quattlebaum, 2 Bail. 452 ; Fox v. McGregor, 11 Barb. 41.

[2] Cross on Lien, p. 30 ; Snead v. Watkins, 1 Com. B. N. S. 267.

[3] Byall v. ——, Atk. 165. See, also, Chapter VII.

[4] Manning v. Hollenbeck, 27 Wis. 202.

[5] Dicas v. Stockley, 7 Car. & P. 587 ; Bristol v. Wilsmore, 1 Barn. & C. 514.

[6] Ratcliff v. Davies, Cro. Jac. 244.

[7] Gordon v. Cox, 7 Car. & P. 172.

[8] Per Willes. J., Allen v. Smith, 12 Com. B. N. S. 644.

"Must the man say why he refuses to give up the goods?"

"If he gives a reason for detaining them other than his right of lien, he waives that, and it is gone; still, merely omitting to mention it when the goods are demanded will not prevent him enforcing it."[1]

"Could not a guest get off by paying a small sum on account?"

"No; for then a farthing in cash would destroy the right;[2] but taking a note payable at a future day will put a stop to it."[3]

"I believe that the landlord cannot sell the goods seized," suggested my comrade.

"No, except by consent or operation of law."[4]

"Is there no limit to the amount for which the lien can exist?"

"That point was disposed of in a case where a young fellow's mother asked a hotel-keeper not to allow her son, who was a guest in the house, more than a certain quantity of brandy and water per diem, yet mine host supplied the youth with considerably more of that beverage than was named. When the bill was disputed, the judge held that a landlord was not bound to examine the nature of the articles ordered by a guest before he supplied them; but might furnish whatever was ordered, and that the guest was bound to pay for them, pro-

---

[1] Owen v. Knight, 5 Scott, 307.
[2] Hodgson v. Loy, 7 T. R. 660.
[3] Horncastle v. Farran, 2 Barn. & Ald. 497.
[4] Case v. Fogg, 46 Mo. 66; Thames Iron W. Co. v. Patent Derrick Co. 1 Johns. & W. 97; Mulliner v. Florence L. R. 3 Q. B. 484.

vided he was possessed of reason, and not an infant."[1]

"Oh, then, a juvenile's goods and chattels cannot be kept for his little hotel bill? Another privilege gone forever with the happy days of childhood," said De Gex.

"I am not quite so sure. In Kentucky, it was held that they could be, if the entertainment was furnished in good faith, without the knowledge that the youngster was acting improperly and contrary to the wishes of his guardian; and it was even held that the innkeeper had a lien for money given to the boy and expended by him for necessaries,"[2] I remarked.

"I trust," said my companion, "that there is not very much more to be said on the subject. I feel that I am growing thin, and will soon require a lean-to to support me."

"You are like the rest of the world, ingrate and thankless. Here I have been giving you freely of what has cost me long, weary hours of study and gallons of petroleum, and still you grumble. Only two points more would I endeavor to impress upon your memory, the knowledge of which may prove to be worth to you fully the cost of this drive of ours."

"Well, I will restrain myself and lend a listening ear."

"In the first place, if an innkeeper should retain your trunks for your hotel bill, you need pay him

[1] Proctor v. Nicholson, 7 Car. & P. 67.
[2] Watson v. Cross, 2 Duv. (Ken.) 147.

nothing for his trouble in taking care of them there-
after; when you are flush again, you may call, and
on paying the original amount due, demand your
traps.[1] In that way, you see, you may sometimes
get rid of the trouble of carrying your baggage
about with you. Then, again, whenever possible,
travel in company, with all the baggage in one
trunk; let the one who owns the trunk pay his
bill, and then all may go on their way rejoicing;
for where a paterfamilias took his daughters to
an hotel and the board of all was charged to the
old man, (who afterward became insolvent) it was
well decided that the trunks of one of the girls
could not be detained for the whole amount due
by the party. Every man for himself, seems to be
the rule."[2]

"What are you two men gossiping about?"
suddenly broke in Mrs. Lawyer, she and her companion having fully exhausted their stock of chit-
chat.

"Gossiping!" said De Gex; "no indeed; as Sir
Boyle Roche would say, I deny the allegation,
and defy the allegator."

"None with a properly constituted mind would
indulge in such a thing; for George Eliot well
defines gossip to be ' a sort of smoke which comes
from the dirty tobacco-pipes of those who diffuse
it,' and remarks that it proves nothing but the bad
taste of the smoker," I added.

[1] Somes v. British Emp. Sh. Co. 8 H. L. Cas. 338; El. B. & E.
353. But see, in cases of horses, p. 129.
[2] Clayton v. Butterfield, 10 Rich. 423.

The ladies seemed conscience-stricken, for neither replied, and for some time we all sat in silence, enjoying the delicious coolness of eventide; each was busied in private castle-building, or "watching out the light of sunset, and the opening of that bead-roll which some oriental poet describes as God's call to the little stars, who each answer, 'Here am I!'"

Chapter IX.

DUTIES OF A BOARDING-HOUSE KEEPER.

Suns had risen and set; moons had waxed and
waned, and Mrs. Lawyer and myself were now
settled in a boarding-house. I will not say comfortably, for, although never in my youth did I
own a little hatchet, still I have read in my younger
days the fifth chapter of the Acts of the Apostles.

My powers of description are exceedingly limited,
so I will not attempt to sketch, for the benefit of
my readers, either the house itself, its furnishings,
its occupants, or the entertainment provided as a
quid pro their dollars. Of the furniture, I will only
say that the carpet on the parlor floor " was bediz-
ened like a Ricaree Indian—all red chalk, yellow
ochre, and cock's feathers." Of our fellow boarders,
'tis sufficient to remark that some, on one or two
occasions, had, perhaps, worn kid gloves; most of
the men were " self-made, whittled into shape with
their own jack-knives"; the ladies—but *de feminis
nil nisi bonum.*

Of the food provided for the inner man, need
more be said than that the poultry, which appeared
on the second day of our sojourn, would have seemed
to Mr. Baguet's fastidious eye, suitable for Mrs. B.'s
birthday dinner? If there be any truth in adages,
they certainly were not caught by chaff. Every
kind of finer tendon and ligament that it is in the

nature of poultry to possess, was developed in these specimens in the singular form of guitar strings. Their limbs appeared to have struck roots into their breasts and bodies, as aged trees strike roots into the earth. Their legs were so hard as to encourage the idea that they must have devoted the greater part of their long and arduous lives to pedestrian exercises and the walking of matches. No one could have cleaned the drum-sticks without being of ostrich descent."

Ab uno disce omnes. Ex pede Herculem. From these three hints let each one, for himself, erect images of our boarding-house, our fellow-boarders, and our meals, as a Cuvier would reconstruct a me-gatherium from a tooth, or an Agassiz draw a pic-ture of an unknown fish from a single scale. But I must not dip my pen in vinegar, nor tip it with wormwood, when I write of boarding-houses and their industrious and unfortunate keepers. These providers of food and lodging seem to be the de-scendants of Ishmael, their hand being against every one to eke out their little profits, and every one's hand being against them. Let me be an honorable exception to the general rule, and act like the Good Samaritan, although, by the way, that worthy patronized a cheap hotel, not a boarding-house.

* * * * *

It has ever been a hobby of mine that a door— hall or otherwise—is intended to be shut (if not, a hole in the wall would answer every purpose and be cheaper). Well, one great source of trouble with me at Madame Dee's private boarding-house was that the domestic-of-all-work was in the constant habit of leaving the hall door ajar whenever she made her exit on to the street in her hunt for butter, eggs, or milk. A fellow-boarder, seeing my anxiety on this point, asked me if I was afraid of some one stealing Mrs. Lawyer.

"No," I replied, "I am more afraid of my overcoat. Although not very new, it is still serviceable."

"Well, sir," said a youthful reader of Blackstone and Story, "if any one feloniously and wickedly takes away your bad habit could you not deduct the value of it on your next week's settlement with Mrs. Dee? An innkeeper would be liable in such a case."

"My dear young friend," I replied, "you have as yet acquired only the A B C of professional knowledge. The liability of a boarding - house keeper for the goods of a boarder is by no means the same as that of an innkeeper."

Here I paused, but-the first speaker asked me to proceed and explain the difference, so I spake somewhat as follows:

"Once upon a time Catherine Dansey went to the boarding-house of Elizabeth F. Richardson with her luggage, and was duly received within the mansion. One day some of Mrs. Dansey's goods, chattels, or knick-knacks were stolen, and when the matter was investigated it appeared that the thief had entered through the front door—which had been left open by the servant—and that

Mrs. Richardson knew that her Biddy was in the constant habit of neglecting to shut the door. Mrs. R. would not settle the affair amicably, so Mrs. D. had the law of her.[1] At the trial the judge told the jury that a boarding-house keeper was bound to take due and reasonable care about the safe-keeping of a guest's goods; and then, it having struck his lordship that perhaps his twelve enlightened countrymen, who sat before him in the box, did not know too well what due care might be, he proceeded to explain to them that it was such care as a prudent housekeeper would take in the management of his own house for the protection of his own goods. The judge went on to say that Mrs. Richardson's servant leaving the door open might be a want of such care, but the mistress was not answerable for such negligence, unless she herself had been guilty of some neglect (as in keeping such a servant with a knowledge of her habits). The jury, as in duty bound, took the law from his lordship and said that Dame R. was not liable."

"Then Mrs. Dansey had to perform to the tune of a nice little bill of costs, and grin and bear it," remarked the embryo Coke.

"She was rather stubborn about it, and applied for a new trial."

"Did she get it?" asked Coke *in futuro.*

"No. The whole four judges gave it as their opinion that a boarding-house keeper is not bound to keep a guest's baggage safely to the same extent as an innkeeper, but that the law implies an under-

[1] Dansey v. Richardson, 3 El. & Bl. 144.

taking on his part to take due and proper care of
the boarder's belongings, although nothing was said
about it; and that neglecting to take due care of
an outer door might be a breach of such duty."

"But did they say what due and proper care
amounted to?" was queried.

"Yes; but, as doctors often do, they disagreed
on the point. Judge Wightman could not see that
a boarding-house keeper is a bailee of the goods of
his guest at all, or that he is bound to take more
care of them (when they are no further given into
his care than by being in his house) than he as a
prudent man would take of his own. If he were
guilty of negligence in the selection of his servants,
or in keeping such as he might well distrust, his
lordship said that he could hardly be considered as
taking the care of a prudent owner, and so might
be liable for a loss occasioned by a servant's neglect. Erle, J., said that as there was no delivery of
the goods by Mrs. D. to Mrs. R., no contract to
keep them with care and deliver them again, and
nothing paid in respect of the goods, there was no
duty of keeping them placed upon Richardson.
Judge Coleridge and Lord Campbell looked at the
case through spectacles of another color — the former said that a guest at such a house is entitled to
due and reasonable care absolutely; he comes to
the house and pays his money for certain things to
be rendered in return; he stipulates directly with
the master, having no control himself over the servants, and having nothing to do with the master's
judiciousness or care or good fortune in selecting

them; and the master undertakes to the guest not merely to be careful in the choice of his servants, but absolutely to take due and reasonable care of his goods.   Lord Campbell said that he could not go so far as to say that in no case can a boarding-house keeper be liable for the loss of goods through the negligence of a servant, although he himself was guiltless of any negligence in hiring or keeping the domestic.   If one employs servants to keep the outer door shut when there is danger of thieves, while they are performing that duty they are acting within the scope of their employment, and he is answerable for their negligence.   He is not answerable for the consequences of a felony, or even a willful trespass committed by them; but the general rule is, that the master is responsible for the negligence of his servants while engaged in offices which he employs them to do—and his lordship (for I have been quoting his sentiments) said that he was not aware how the keeper of a board-ing house could be an exception to the general rule."

I stopped here, and was rather chagrined to catch one of those present saying to another—

"Do you remember what old Coates said about his wife?"

"No—what?"

" 'M-Mrs. C-Coates is a f-funny old watch.   She b-broke her chain a g-good while ago, and has been r-running down ever since; she must have a main-spring a mile long.'   This is apropos of our friend here when he gets started on a legal point."

"And he is always starting some such shoppy subject; like Adelaide Proctor's young man —

'He cracks no egg without a legal sigh,
    Nor eats of beef but thinking on the law,' "

was the response wafted into the recesses of my auricular appendages — so chilling it was that I incontinently sneezed thrice.

"There seems," said the student, "to have been a decided diversity of opinion among the learned judges in that case."

"Yes, indeed," I replied. "But the point has been made clear in a more recent case, in which all the judges took the same view of the extent of the liability."

" What was that decision, sir ? "

" That the law imposes no obligation on a lodging-house keeper to take care of the goods of his boarder. A lodger who was just about to change his quarters, was out of his room, and the landlord allowed a stranger to enter to look at it; the latter carried off some of the boarder's property, and when the owner sued the landlord the court gave him to understand that he must himself bear the loss. Earle, C. J., said that the judges had decided that even if the things had been stolen by a member of the household the proprietor would not be liable. He went on to remark that he was most particularly averse to affirming, for the first time, that a lodging-house keeper has the duty cast upon him of taking care of his guest's goods ; he saw great difficulties

1 Holder *v.* Soulby, 8 C. B. N. S. 254.

in so holding, and thought it would be casting upon him an undefined responsibility which would be most inconvenient; considering that lodgers consist of all classes—from the highest to the lowest—one could hardly exaggerate the mischief that would ensue from holding the proprietor liable. It would be impossible, his lordship continued, to lay down any definite test of liability; each case must be left to the discretion or caprice of a jury; the liability of the keeper of the house must vary according to the situation of the premises and a variety of circumstances too numerous to mention. If, on the other hand, the law is that the lodger must take care of his own goods, it only imposes upon him the same care which he is bound to take when he walks the streets ; he may always secure his valuables by carrying them about with him, or by placing them specially in the custody of the keeper of the house."

"But it appears rather hard to compel a man to carry his goods about with him wherever he goes, or else hand them over to the boarding-house keeper who might be down in the kitchen cooking dinner or washing cups and saucers; besides, she or he might refuse to take care of them," captiously remarked one of the company.

"Notwithstanding all that, I have told you the law correctly, and Byles, J., remarked once that a contrary decision would cast upon the proprietor ' a frightful amount of liability,' " I replied.

"Did the judges in the case you just referred to say anything about the open door case?" questioned the earnest inquirer after knowledge.

"Yes, and held that the whole tenor of the judgment in it was that a boarding-house keeper is not bound to take such reasonable degree of care of the goods of his guest as a prudent man may reasonably be expected to take of his own."

"It seems strange," urged the youth—by the way, a careless, heedless young fellow was he—"that such people should in no way be liable to look after the property of their boarders."

"I did not say exactly that. They are of course liable where a loss of a lodger's goods has resulted from gross negligence on their part, or they themselves have been guilty of some misdeed."[1]

"Those two cases, I think," said one who had been a silent listener hitherto, "were both decided in England; but what say our American judges on the point?"

"So far as they have spoken," I replied, "they have, as a rule, corroborated and agreed with the sentiments of their ermined and bewigged fellows across the ocean. The Supreme Court of Tennessee decided that an innkeeper was not liable for the clothing of a boarder stolen from his room, without the former's fault, although he would be for that of a guest;[2] and the judge gave as his reason for making the distinction that a passenger or wayfaring man may be an entire stranger in the place, and must put up and lodge at the inn to which his day's journey may bring him, and so it is important that he should be protected by the most stringent

[1] Idem—Earle, C. J.
[2] Manning v. Wells, 9 Humph. 746.

rules of law enforcing the liability of hotel-keepers;
but as a boarder does not need such protection the
law does not afford it, and it is sufficient to give him
a remedy when he proves the innkeeper guilty of
culpable neglect. And in Kentucky, where a regular boarder at an hotel deposited gold with the proprietor, who put it in his safe, into which thieves
broke and stole, the court held that the hotel-
keeper was not liable as an innkeeper, but only as a
depositary without reward, and as no gross negligence was shown the poor boarder failed in his attempt to recover his lost cash in that way.[1] I had
better tell you, however, that in New York it has
very recently been held that a boarding-house
keeper is liable for the loss of a boarder's property
by theft, committed by a stranger allowed to enter
the boarder's room by a servant of the house,[2] and
that it is his duty to exercise such care over a boarder's goods as a prudent man would over his own."

"Well, will you please tell me what is the difference between a boarding-house and an inn?" asked
one of the other boarders.

"It would afford me great pleasure to answer
your question at another time, but at the present I
am sorry to say that duty calls me and I must go."

Leaving my listeners to digest the law lecture I
had delivered to them, I repaired to the best parlor, and there found Mrs. Lawyer and another lady
in a state of white heat over the performances of a

[1] Johnson v. Reynolds, 3 Ken. 257. See, also, Chamberlain
v. Masterson, 26 Ala. 371.
[2] Smith v. Reed, 6 Daly, 33.

boarder who occupied the next room—one of the genus referred to by Coleridge when he said,

> "Swans sing before they die ; 'twere no bad thing
> Should certain persons die before they sing "—

who was constantly carolling or trilling with a voice of the most rasping kind, or playing upon a most atrocious accordeon, to the discomfiture and annoyance of the other guests.

" Can that man not be made to keep quiet ? " asked my wife.

"Doubtless, my dear, if you would go and talk to him sweetly, he would cease his songs and lay aside his wind instrument," I gallantly replied.

" Don't tease me," she said.   " Here we both have got splitting headaches through that horrid noise."

" I thought from your manner you seemed a little cracked, my love ; what can I do ? " I queried.

" You ought to know—you are a lawyer; can't you make him stop ? "

" Well, really I don't know.   I remember that in England a man had the constant ringing of a chime of bells in a neighboring chapel stopped on account of the annoyance and discomfort it caused him." [1]

" I am sure that the noise of bells is as heavenly music compared to the infernal discords produced by that man," remarked the other lady, who, like Talmage's friend, Miss Stinger, was sharp as a hornet, prided herself on saying things that cut, could not bear the sight of a pair of pants, loathed a shaving apparatus, and thought Eve would have

[1] Soltan v. De Held, 2 Sim. N. S. 133.

shown a better capacity for housekeeping if she had—the first time she used her broom—swept Adam out of Paradise.

" Yes, dear madam, the noise of belles is often most delightful; and the happiest day of my life was the one on which I was engaged in ringing a sweet village belle, who shall be nameless," I replied, knowing that the lady hated everything like gallantry, and I politely waved my hand towards Mrs. L., who exclaimed :

" You stupid, you ! Tell me directly what we can do ! "

" In the English case I mentioned, the man got an injunction from the Court of Chancery to restrain the noise; but in another case in North Carolina,[1] where a most pious member of a Methodist church was indicted for disturbing divine service by singing in such a way that one part of the congregation laughed, and the other part got mad— the irreligious and frivolous enjoyed it as fun, while the serious and devout were indignant—although the jury found the man guilty, the court reversed the verdict, as the brother did not desire to disturb the worship but was religiously doing his best. So here our poor neighbor is doing what he can to produce a ' concord of sweet sounds.' On another occasion, the judges in the same State held that the noise of a drum or fife in a procession was not a nuisance.[2] But then the wearers of the ermine in that State seem almost indifferent to sounds

[1] State v. Linkham, 69 N. C. 214.
[2] State v. Hughes, 72 N. C. 25.

of any kind; for about the same time, they decided
that profane swearing was not a nuisance, unless it
was loud and long continued." [1]

"What had we better do?" persisted Mrs. Lawyer. "Either he must leave, or we must bid good-
bye to these premises."

"Get the landlady to give him notice to quit;
then if he won't go peaceably, she can bundle him
out neck and crop." [2]

"She will promise to do so, and that will be the
end of it," said the acidulous lady.

"In Massachusetts, where a lodger was disturbed
by the lodger in the room below singing hymns by
no means of the Moody & Sankey style, and the
landlord promised to get the musician out, but
failed to do so, the Supreme Court held that the
aggrieved boarder could not insist upon a diminu-
tion of his weekly bills on account of the disagreeable singing.[3]   But, my dear, will you come and
take a walk with me?"

Off we started countrywards, and——walked.
When we were returning, it was dark and late.
"The night air was soft and balmy; the night odors
sweet and soul-entrancing; there were no listeners
save the grasshoppers and the night-moths with
folded wings among the flower-beds of the cottages,
and no on-lookers save the silent stars and jeweled-
eyed frogs upon the path staring at us" with all
their might and main.   So we gossiped until we

---

[1] State v. Powell, 70 N. C. 67.
[2] Newton v. Harland, 1 M. & G. 644.
[3] De Witt v. Pierson, 112 Mass 8.

entered the city once again, and then the odors
changed ; listeners and lookers-on became numerous ; the stars were eclipsed by flaming gas ; the
frogs gave place to gaping gamins.

*   *   *   *   *   *

As it has to be mentioned, and there is no reason
why it should not be mentioned just here, I may
state (as a hint to those who keep boarders) that
Judge Coleridge once remarked that if a boarding-
house keeper neglected to give a boarder a dry bed
or wholesome food, and in consequence thereof the
latter became sick, it could not be doubted but that
the landlord might be compelled to make compensation in damages to the sufferer. His lordship
also went on to say, in effect, that if the White
Hart Inn, High-street, Borough, had been a boarding-house, and Sam Weller had given the wooden
leg of number six to thirteen, and the pair of Hes-
sians of thirteen to number six ; or the two pairs
of halves of the commercial to the snuggery inside
the bar, and the painted tops of the snuggery to
the commercial, so that any of those worthies had
been damnified, then the bustling old landlady of
that establishment would have had to comfort her
guests in a more substantial manner than she did
when she titillated the nose of the spinster aunt.[1]

[1] Dansey v. Richardson, 3 El. & B. 144.

Chapter X.

MORE ABOUT BOARDING-HOUSE KEEPERS.

Again it was night. All the boarders were assembled around the tea-table; not exactly, however, as Dr. Talmage would wish, for he said that you should be seated wide enough apart to have room to take out your handkerchief if you want to cry at any pitiful story, or to spread yourself in laughter if some one propound an irresistible conundrum.

The tea was none of that good old stuff that once brought $50 a pound, but some of the adulterated mixture, thirty million pounds of which Uncle Sam, Aunt Columbia and their little ones, pour annually into their saucers and empty into their mouths.

"Now, then, Mr. Lawyer," said my friend Mr. Jim Crax, as the bread and butter, tea and toast were fast disappearing off the table on to the chairs, "kindly redeem your promise, and tell us the difference between a boarding-house keeper and an hotel-keeper; that is, the difference in law—we all know the practical differences only too well."

After a preliminary hem and haw, I began as follows: "It might be as well to say, in the first place, that a boarding-house is not in common parlance, or in legal meaning, every private house where one or more boarders are occasionally kept upon special considerations; but is a *quasi*-public

house, where boarders are generally and habit-
ually received as a matter of business, and which
is held out to the public and known as a place
of entertainment of that kind.[1] The chief distinction between a boarding-house and an inn, and
the one from which all others naturally flow, is
that the keeper of a boarding-house can choose his
own guests, admitting some and rejecting others, as
to him in his discretion or according to his whims
and humors may seem best; while an innkeeper is
obliged to entertain all travelers of good conduct,
and possessed of means of payment, who choose
to stop at his house, and those who do stay he must
provide with all they have occasion for while on
their way."[2]

"That seems rather hard on the innkeeper."

"No: he is compensated by having greater privileges than his humbler brother; and such a rule is
necessary for the welfare and convenience of the
traveling public, who cannot be expected, in the
hurry of journeyings, to stop and hunt through a
town for a night's lodging, making a special bargain
with the keeper of the house. A lodging-house
keeper makes a special contract with every man
that comes to him, whereas an innkeeper is bound,
without any particular agreement, to provide lodging and entertainment for all who come to him, at
a reasonable price.[3] In the one case the guest is
entertained on an implied contract from day to day;

[1] Cady v. McDowell, 1 Lans. (N. Y.) 484.
[2] Pinkerton v. Woodward, 33 Cal. 557.
[3] Thompson v. Lacy, 3 Barn. & Adol. 283

in the other, there is an express contract for a certain time at a certain rate."[1]

"But surely," said Jim Crax, "oftentimes a definite agreement to board is made with an hotel-keeper."

"Of course, I know that," I replied. "But, then, if he does so on the arrival of his guest he loses the rights and privileges as well as the liabilities of his order; although an arrangement as to the price only, after one has become a guest, will not have that effect.[2]   And it has been held that a public hotel at a watering place possessing medicinal springs, and opened only during the summer and fall for the accommodation of visitors in search of health and pleasure, is, in fact, only a boarding-house, the visitors not being guests for a day, night, or week, but lodgers or boarders for a season."[3]

"What," said the landlady's daughter, who was angling for the young law student and so tried to season her generally frivolous conversation with an occasional semi-sensible remark or question, "What are the privileges of an innkeeper which a boarding-house keeper does not enjoy? The right to charge $5 per day?"

"Their right of lien. You, of course, know what that is?" I replied.

"Oh, certainly," she answered, though she no more knew what it meant than I do the hieroglyphics on Cleopatra's Needle.

[1] Willard v. Reinhardt, 2 E. D. Smith, 148.

[2] Wharton on Innkeepers, 123.

[3] Benner v. Welburn, 7 Ga. 296, 307; Southwood v. Myers, 3 Bush, 681.

"I don't," said a lady with greater honesty. "But pray, don't attempt to define it. I never try to find out the meaning of a word since I once looked in Johnson's dictionary and found that network was 'anything reticulated or decussated with interstices between the intersections.'"

"I thought that the proprietor of a boarding-house also had the right of detaining the goods of their lodgers for their charges," remarked the seediest of the company who looked as if he had had practical experience in such matters.

"Not generally; although in some States the legislatures have conferred the right upon them to the same extent as an innkeeper has at common law. This they have, for instance, in New York, New Hampshire, and Wisconsin;[1] and in Connecticut they have not only the right to retain the property until the debt is paid, but in case of non-payment they can sell it to recoup themselves after a certain time."[2]

"Suppose," said the student, " as is the case here, one who keeps boarders occasionally entertains travelers for a night or so—would she be considered an hotel-keeper in respect to those stray sheep?"

"No," I replied.

"How would it be if a man agreed to go to a boarding-house and then backed out and went elsewhere?" asked my *vis-a-vis* at the table.

[1] Stewart *v.* McCready, 24 How. Pr. 62; Jones *v.* Merrill, 42 Barb. 623; Cross *v.* Wilkins, 43 N. H. 332; Nichols *v.* Holliday, 29 Wis. 406.

[2] Brooks *v.* Harrison, 41 Conn. 184.

15.

"Well, where a man of the name of Stewart agreed by word of mouth with one who took boarders to pay £100 a year for the board and lodging of himself and servant and the keep of his horse, and then failed to take up his quarters at the house, the court considered that the bargain was not a contract concerning land within the Statute of Frauds and so did not require to be in writing, and that Stewart was liable to pay for the breach of his agreement." [1]

"What is that in front of you, sir?" was queried of me.

"Pork chops, apparently," I replied. "Will you take one?"

"No, thanks; I am a Jew as far as pork is concerned. In fact, although not so bad as Marshal d'Albert, who was always taken ill whenever he saw a roast sucking-pig, I am like the celebrated Guianerius—pork always gives me a violent palpitation of the heart."

"'Tis curious what antipathies some people have to particular kinds of food. I have read of a man who was always seized with a fit when he tried to swallow a piece of meat," said a Mr. Knowall.

"Nature evidently intended him for a vegetarian."

"I have heard of another who was made ill if he ever ate any mutton," continued the gentleman; "and of a man who always had an attack of the gout a few hours after eating fish. In fact, the celebrated Erasmus could not smell fish without being thrown

---

[1] Wright v. Stewart, 29 Law J. Q. B. 161.

into a fever; Count d'Armstadt never failed to go off in a faint if he knowingly or unknowingly partook of any dish containing the slightest modicum of olive oil; the learned Scaliger would shudder in every limb on beholding water-cresses; and Vladisiaus, of Poland, would fly at the sight of apples."

"I read once of a lady who, if she ventured to taste lobster salad at a dancing party, would, before she could return to the ball-room, be covered with ugly blotches and her peace of mind destroyed for that evening," I remarked.

"The whole question of food is an interesting one," said Mr. Knowall.

"Do you mean with regard to the sumptuary laws of other days?" queried the law student.

"Yes. You remember that in the days of the Plantagenets the Houses of Parliament solemnly resolved that no man, of what state or condition soever he might be, should have at dinner or supper, or any other time, more than two courses, and each of two sorts of victual at the utmost, be it of flesh or fish, with the common sorts of potage, without sauce or any sort of victuals. And the eating of flesh of any kind during Lent and on Fridays and Saturdays, was punished by a fine of ten shillings, or imprisonment for ten days;[1] and in the days of Queen Bess the fine was increased to £3 and the term of imprisonment to three months; but if any one had three dishes of sea-fish on his table he might have one of flesh also."[2]

[1] 2 and 3 Edw. VI, chap. 19.   [2] 5 Eliz. chap. 5, sec. 15.

"Did Elizabeth do this from any religious mo-
tive?" asked a young divine.

"Oh, dear, no. The statute expressly says that
the eating of fish is not necessary for the saving of
the soul of man. In the days of bluff old King
Hal, Archbishop Cranmer commanded that no cler-
gyman should have more than three blackbirds in a
pie unless he was a bishop and then he might have
four, but he allowed himself and his brother of
York to have six."

"When then, pray, did the fashion of having
'four-and-twenty blackbirds baked in a pie' come
into vogue?" asked my wife, who had a good
memory for infantile rhymes.

CHAPTER XI.

CHARMS OF FURNISHED APARTMENTS.

"*De gustibus non est disputandum,*" was originally observed by a man of sense, however many blockheads may since have repeated it; and as my tastes in the matter of comestibles did not harmonize with those of the several respectable boarding-house keepers beneath whose roofs we successively took shelter, it was settled in a committee of the whole family that Mrs. Lawyer and myself should take furnished apartments in a genteel street, or a furnished house—that Mrs. L. should be appointed Commissary-General, with one Bridget or Biddy O'Callaghan as Deputy-Acting-Assistant Commissary-General under her, while I should continue to hold the responsible post of Paymaster-General to the entire force.

In due time, after a considerable reduction in our stock of the virtue of patience and of the thickness of the soles of our boots, a suitable suite of rooms, furnished in a style agreeable to our taste, in a locality not objectionable and at a rate proportionate to the depth or rather shallowness of my pocket, was discovered and all necessary arrangements made with the landlord.

To avoid all possibility of future disputations with the owner, (and especially as a contract to let lodgings is a contract concerning an interest in land within the meaning of that celebrated troublesome statute passed in the twenty-ninth year of his rascally majesty, Charles II, and entitled "an act for the prevention of frauds and perjuries," and so must be in writing,[1]) I determined to follow the good advice of Mr. Woodfall, and have our agreement reduced to black and white. My instructions to my clerk in preparing the document were, to specify the amount of rent, the time of entry, the length of notice to quit required and such other particulars as the nature of the case rendered requisite, and to have a list of the goods and chattels in the apartments affixed.

Alas, I found the truth of the old adage, that a lawyer who acts for himself has a —— well, not a Solomon — for his client. An unexpected event, however, saved me. The very evening before we were to enter into our new abode a bailiff, on behalf of the real owner, for my acquaintance had but a lease of the place, visited the house and seized a part of the furniture for rent overdue; luckily none of my personal belongings had been taken in—if there had been any of them they, too, would have been liable to distress for the rent. I had stupidly neglected to inquire whether the taxes or the rent of the house were paid up, and whether they were likely to be kept so.[2] Of course I knew that if I had at that particular period of my existence chanced to have been living in New England,

---

[1] Woodfall, Landlord and Tenant. But see Wright *v.* Stewart, 6 Jur. N. S. 867.
[2] Woodfall, Landlord and Tenant. But see Wright *v.* Stewart, 6 Jur. N. S. 867.

or in New York State, or in some of the other
States of the Union, I could not have been troubled
if in that house, as the power of distress exists in
those places no longer;[1] but we were in a State in
which it is still retained, or at least was then.

When I told my wife of the narrow escape we
had had she asked me if I had ever made inquiries
as to whether the landlords of the hotels at which
we stayed were in arrear for rent.

"No," I replied; "the rule is different in respect
to hotels."

"Why?"

"For the benefit of trade; otherwise business
could not be carried on at all."

"But what would we have had there except my
cat and bird, our clothes, and your books?" urged
Mrs. L.

"Nothing more would have been wanted."

"Could they have taken our clothes? I thought
all such things were exempt."

"Generally speaking, they are from seizure for
debt; but not from distress for rent, unless they
are in actual use at the time. In 1796 Mr. Baynes,
who had furnished lodgings at half a guinea a week,
was two months in arrear, and a bailiff appeared
upon the scene and took his wearing apparel and
that of Mrs. B., although part of it was actually in
the wash-tub at the time; and Lord Kenyon said it
was all right.[2] The same judge decided in another
case that a landlord could legally take the clothes

[1] Parsons on Contracts, vol. 1, p. 517.
[2] Baynes v. Smith, 1 Esp. 206.

belonging to a man's wife and children, while they
—the 'clothes screens,' as Carlyle calls them—not
the clothes—were in bed, although the bipeds intended to put them on in the morning, and had been
daily in the habit of wearing them, on the ground
that they were not in actual use.[1]   But Kenyon, my
dear, sometimes said absurd things.   For instance,
once, when indignant at the delay of an attorney,
he exclaimed, wrathfully, 'This is the last hair in
the tail of procrastination.'"

"The law seems very hard.   Why, that poor
woman would have to stay in bed.   But talking of
tails, could they have taken my cat—my beautiful pussy?" said Mrs. Lawyer, looking over where

> The cat's dark silhouette on the wall,
> A couchant tiger's seemed to fall.

"Well—ah—in Coke upon Littleton it is said,
no; but the reason given is that cats are things in
which no man can have an absolute and valuable
property; and that reason might not be applicable
to the case of a costly Angora like yours, and you
know, *cessante ratione cessat et ipsa lex;* but your
bird might have been taken."[2]

"It seems strange that the landlord can take the
property of other people to pay his tenant's debts."

"It does; and in many parts of this country only
the goods of the debtor can be taken,[3] and the
judges are generally inclined to deliver the lodger

---

[1] Bisset *v*. Caldwell, 1 Esp. 206, *n*.
[2] Woodfall, Landlord and Tenant, 384.
[3] Parsons on Contracts, vol. 1, p. 518.

from the claws of the landlord; and so it has been held that while the goods of an assignee of the tenant are liable, those of a mere under-tenant are not;[1] and in England, of late years, an act has been passed for the protection of the lodger's goods from the claims of the landlord for rent due him by his immediate tenant."[2]

"But if our things had been taken to pay the rent, could we not have made the other boarders contribute their share?"

"No, I am afraid not,"[3] I answered.

*   *   *   *   *

Our intended rooms being now somewhat de-nuded of their necessary furnishings we arranged with our landlord-about-to-be to send in all neces-sary articles within a reasonable time. Unfortu-nately, however, this new arrangement was not em-bodied in our written agreement; so I found out— when too late—that our landlord (a man of the eel kind) was not bound to put in the furniture. If it had been in writing, it would then have formed an inseparable part of the contract, and the man could not have obtained his rent until he had done his duty.[4]

We had scarcely got settled in our new quarters before we discovered that our rose possessed a thorn or two. The morning after our arrival, we

---

[1] Archer *v*. Wetherell, 4 Hill (N. Y.) 112.

[2] 34 and 35 Vict. chap. 79; Phillips *v*. Henson, L. R. 3 C P. D. 26.

[3] Hunter *v*. Hunt, 1 Com. B. 300.

[4] Mechelen *v*. Wallace, 7 Ad. & E. 49; Vaughan *v*. Han-cock, 3 Com. B. 766.

were honored with the visit of a choleric gent,
who informed us that he occupied the rooms on
the flat below and that our water pipes had leaked
through and damaged irreparably some of his
property. I am thankful, however, to say that I
was able to point out to him that the defects in the
pipe could not have been detected without exami-
nation; that as we did not know of them, and had
not been guilty of any negligence, we were not
liable for the damage which he had unfortunately
sustained, there being no obligation upon us to
keep—at our peril—the water in the pipe.[1]

We next had trouble about a stovepipe which
had to pass through another person's room. When
we began to put it up our neighbor threatened to
take it down and stop up the hole; but knowing
that as there had been a pipe through his room before the surly fellow moved in he only had the
room subject to the easement of the stovepipe and
hole,[2] I remained firm and steadfast, and finally won
a way for the obnoxious, black, cylindrical smoke-
conductor, and we hoped to hear the kettle sing
merrily, and the pots bubble, and spirt, and boil in
peace, if not in quietude.

But our triumph was not for long. Barely was
the stove in full blast when the boiler attached exploded with a terrific uproar. Considerable damage was done; my wife was clamorous that I should
at once interview the landlord, especially as we
thought that the accident could not have happened

[1] Ross v. Fedden, 7 Q. B. 661.
[2] Culverwell v. Lockington, 24 C. P. (Ont.' 611.

had there been a safety-valve to the boiler; but I said that it would be useless to talk about it unless we could prove that he knew of the defect, or had reason to suspect it, or that damage was to be apprehended from the use of the boiler for the purpose for which it was intended;[1] although on one occasion the courts held a landlord liable for injuries arising from the explosion of gas, caused by the pipes in the tenant's room not having been properly secured.[2]

In the afternoon it began to rain in the style commonly called "cats and dogs," or "pitchforks," and soon we heard pit—pit—pit, patter—patter—patter, spit—spit—spit, spatter—spatter—spatter, sounding nearer than the dripping outside would seem to warrant, and on investigation we found that the rain was coming through the roof and dropping down in ugly splashes upon one of our most handsome and costly volumes.

"Can we make the landlord pay for the damage done by his old leaky roof?" asked my wife, as with her best cambric handkerchief she tried to swab up the wet.

"I fear me not. I remember Baron Martin saying that one who takes a floor in a house must be held to take the premises as they are, and cannot complain that the house was not constructed differently. This storm may have blown off some shingles, and then, even if our landlord is bound to use reasonable care in keeping the roof secure, he

---

[1] Jaffe v. Harteau, 56 N. Y. 398.
[2] Kimmell v. Burfiend, 2 Daly (N. Y.), 155.

cannot be held responsible for what no reasonable
care and vigilance could have provided against.
He cannot certainly be considered guilty of negligence if he has caused the roof to be examined
periodically, and if it was all secure the last time it
was looked at.[1]   Still, in New York State it was
decided that where a landlord, who himself occupied an upper flat, allowed liquids to leak through
into his tenants' rooms, he was liable."[2]

"I should think, indeed, that a man should keep
his house in repair, so that his tenants' goods are
not ruined," indignantly said Mrs. Lawyer.

"You may say that, but the law says quite the
reverse. It is perfectly clear that a landlord is not
bound to do any repairs, however necessary they
may be, except such as he personally agrees to do.
The law will not imply any contract of that sort on
his part. That was decided in a case where large
gaps opened in the main walls, and it took several
hours of hard pumping daily to keep the water out
of the basement.[3]

"In New Hampshire, I admit, it has been held
that where a landlord negligently constructs his
building, or negligently allows it to continue out of
repair, he is liable for injuries to his tenants;[4] and
in New York the rule is said to be that when buildings are in good repair when leased and afterward

[1] Carstairs v. Taylor, L. R. 6 Ex. 223.
[2] Stapenhurst v. Am. Man. Co. 15 Abb. Pr. N. S. 355; Simon-
ton v. Loring, 68 Me. 164.
[3] Arden v. Pullen, 10 Mees. & W. 321; Keates v. Cadogan,
10 C. B. 591; Gott v. Gandy, 2 El. & B. 845; Wiltz v. Matthews,
52 N. Y. 512; Taffe v. Harteau, 56 N. Y. 398.
[4] Scott v. Simons, 54 N. H. 426.

become ruinous and dangerous, the owner is not responsible unless he has expressly agreed to repair."[1]

"Surely, then, one has not to pay rent when a house is in such a wretched state? I suppose we are not bound to stay here."

"Yes, to both your queries. The only cases in which a tenant has been permitted to withdraw from his tenancy and refuse payment of rent are where there has been some error or fraudulent misdescription of the premises, or where they have been found to be uninhabitable in consequence of the wrongful act or default of the landlord himself;[2] and it is not perfectly clear that he can do so even then.[3] But I must go out for the present, my dear. Fare thee well."

In the hall down stairs I met Mr. Screwhard, our landlord, a gentleman who, from his personal appearance, would have accumulated a large fortune as an undertaker; for from his countenance you could no more have coaxed a smile than you could have out of a poker. As I was bidding him a hurried "Good morning," he placed his body, so long, so lean, and so straight that you might have taken it for a telegraph pole in consumption, before me, and said, in tones which would have well become the ghost in Hamlet —

"You must be in by nine o'clock, sir; we lock the front door then."

[1] Clancy v. Byrne, 56 N. Y. 129.
[2] Izon v. Gorton, 5 Bing. N. C. 501; 7 Scott, 537.
[3] Surplice v. Farnsworth, 7 M. & G. 576.

"Gammon!" said I; "you will have to unlock it, then, to let me in; for when you rented me the rooms you impliedly granted all that was necessary for their free use and full enjoyment, such as the use of the hall and stairs whenever required, and not only when you choose."[1]

"I will yield to your wishes for this night only," said Screwhard, in a voice as solemn as if he were about to be cremated; "but mind, rap with your knuckles on the door; in time your wife will hear and can let you in, for I must be allowed to have unbroken slumbers; my health demands that most imperatively."

"Stuff and nonsense!" I replied; "I have a right to use the bell and the knocker, as nothing was said to the contrary before;[2] and I shall use them."

And impatient with the old fellow I passed on, saying to myself: "The man must be a fool. An action will lie against him if he attempts to interfere with our use of the necessary adjuncts of his furnished apartments. To be sure if we were bad tenants, he might, in mitigation of damages, show that he acted so to make us leave.[3] But we have not been long enough for that."

Apollo stayed not his fiery steeds in their downward career towards the happy isles of the west that day, and Phœbus' sickly-looking sister held sway in high heaven when I again reached the door

---

[1] Maclennan v. Royal Ins. Co. 39 Q. B. (Ont.) 515.
[2] Underwood v. Burrows, 7 Car. & P. 26.
[3] Idem.

of my new domicile. With me was Tom Jones,
who was anxious to see the rooms. Mrs. Lawyer
received us in the parlor with a face full of disgust,
and after the interchange of a word or two with
Tom, calling me aside, made the hórrid announce-
ment that our bedrooms were fully occupied by animals of a small size, broad for their length, darkish
in color, scented, anthropophagous, and designated
by the same letters as very dark drawing pencils.

I disclosed the fact to T. J., who, being somewhat
of a naturalist, might, I thought, be able to prescribe
some cure for this new found evil. He at once exclaimed :

" I tell you what, old fellow, some scientific folks
say that these creatures always retire from public
life to their own quarters about midnight. Test the
point. You tumble into bed at once, and I will endeavor to entertain Mrs. Lawyer until twelve, and
will call in the morning to hear the result of the
experiment."

" You're very kind, I am sure. But I am always
willing to share things equally with my wife ; besides, when two are in bed the creepers lose time
in deciding which to bite, so one can get occasional
naps. To-morrow we will quit," I replied.

" But can you give up your lodgings in that sum-
mary manner ? "

" Long since it was decided that where a man
rents ready furnished houses or lodgings and they
are infested by bugs, the tenant may leave without
paying rent. Baron Parke, in giving judgment,
said that the authorities appeared fully to warrant

the position that if the demised premises are encum-
bered with a nuisance of so serious a nature that no
person can reasonably be expected to live in them,
the tenant is at liberty to throw them up. And he
said that this was so because of the implied condition that the landlord undertakes to rent the place
in an habitable state. Lord Abinger, in the same
case, went even further, and gave it as his opinion
that no authorities were wanted to establish the
point, and that the case was one which common
sense alone enabled them to decide. A man, he remarked, who lets a ready furnished house, surely
does so under an implied condition, or obligation,
that the house is in a fit state to be inhabited. His
lordship had no doubt whatever on the subject, and
thought that tenants under such circumstances were
fully justified in leaving." [1]

"But have not other equally learned judges had
very grave doubts upon the subject?" queried
Jones.

" Well, I must confess that later cases have
somewhat shaken the authority of the one I have
been referring to, and it has been held that there is
no implied warranty in a lease of a house, or of
land, that it is or shall be reasonably fit for habi-
tation, occupation, or cultivation, and that there is
no contract, still less any condition, implied by law
on the demise of real property only that it is fit
for the purpose for which it is let." [2]

[1] Smith v. Marrable, 11 Mees. & W. 5; Add. on Con. 375–6.
[2] Hart v. Windsor, 11 Mees. & W. 68 ; Sutton v. Temple,
Ibid. 57 ; Searle v. Laverick, Law R. 9 Q. B. 131 ; McGlasham
v. Tallmadge, 37 Barb. 313.

"Does not that put an extinguisher on the authority you cited?" said Jones.

"No; in some of these latter decisions the case of a ready furnished house is expressly distinguished upon the ground that the letting of such a house is a contract of a mixed nature, being in fact a bargain for a house and furniture, which, of necessity, must be such as are fit for the purpose for which they are to be used. Abinger was particularly strong on the point. He said that 'if a party contract for the lease of a house ready furnished, it is to be furnished in a proper manner, and so as to be fit for immediate occupation. Suppose,' said he, 'it turn out that there is not a bed in the house; surely the party is not bound to occupy it or continue in it. So, also, in the case of a house infected with vermin; if bugs be found in the bed, even after entering into possession, the lodger or occupier is not bound to stay in the house. Suppose again,' he continued, 'the tenant discover that there are not sufficient chairs in the house, or that they are not of a sort fit for use: he may give up possession.' [1] And so late as April of the year of grace 1877, Lord C. B. Kelly said that he was of the opinion, both on authority and on general principles of law, that there is an implied condition that a furnished house shall be in a good and tenantable state and reasonably fit for human occupation from the very day on which the tenancy is dated to begin, and that where such a house is in such a condition that there is either great discom-

[1] Hart v. Windsor. *supra.*

fort or danger to health in entering and dwelling
in it, then the intending tenant is entitled to repu-
diate the contract altogether." [1]

"Well, that is strong, I am sure."

"Abinger held that the letting of the goods and
chattels, as well as the house, implies that the party
who lets it so furnished is under an obligation to
supply the other contracting party with whatever
goods and chattels may be fit for the use and occupation of such a house according to its particular
description and suitable in every respect. And
Judge Shaw, of Massachusetts, says that in the
case of furnished rooms in a lodging house, let for
a particular season, a warranty may be implied
that they are suitably fitted for such use." [2]

"I should think," said Jones, "that a would be
tenant ought to go and inspect the premises for
himself."

"If he has an opportunity of doing so it might,
perhaps, make a difference, but if he takes it upon
the faith of its being properly furnished, common
sense and common justice concur in the conclusion
that the owner is bound to let it in an habitable
state. So saith the Lord Chief Baron." [3]

"I believe that it has been held in this country
that the existence of a noxious smell in the house
did not authorize the tenant's leaving." [4]

"Indeed. My lady, the Dowager Countess of

[1] Wilson v. Finch Hatton, L. R. 2 Ex. D. 343.
[2] Dutton v. Gerrish, 63 Mass. 94.
[3] Sutton v. Temple, *supra*.
[4] Westlake v. De Graw, 25 Wend. 669.

Winchelsea, agreed to rent a furnished house in Wilton Crescent, London, for three months of the season of 1875 for the sum of 450 guineas. When her ladyship arrived with her servants and personal luggage, she perceived an unpleasant smell in the house, and declining to occupy it, had her horses taken out of the stable. On investigation, it was found that the drainage was in a very bad state, rendering the house quite unfit for occupation. In three weeks' time, however, matters were put right, but her ladyship refused to go back or to pay rent. A suit was brought, in which the whole court unanimously held that the state of the drains entitled the Countess to rescind the bargain and to refuse to pay rent.[1] Abinger thought that if a tenant, on entering his lodgings, found out that the previous occupier had left because some one had recently died in them of the plague or scarlet fever, he would not be compelled to remain.[2] And in Massachusetts it was decided that a tenant who caught small-pox through no fault of his own, but because the owner wilfully neglected to inform him that the house was infected with that disease, might recover damages from the landlord."[3]

Just then a slight movement on the part of Jones made the chair on which he was perched creak, crack, stretch out its legs, and let him down. As he was hastily apologizing for the damage, I remarked:

[1] Wilson v. Finch Hatton, L. R. 2 Ex. D. 336.
[2] Smith v. Marrable, 11 Mees. & W. 5.
[3] Minor v. Sharon, 112 Mass. 477.

"Don't trouble yourself, the occupier of furnished apartments is not responsible for deterioration by ordinary wear or tear in the reasonable use of the goods of the landlord." [1]

"I'll go now, at all events, as I am up," said our friend, as he seized his hat and made his adieux.

Quære, was that a white handkerchief protruding slightly from his pistol pocket? Indispensables are tighter now-a-days than they used to be.

[1] Add. on Contracts, 377.

Chapter XII.

NOTICE TO QUIT, AND TURNING OUT.

Doubtless many an anxious housekeeper is hurrying rapidly through the pages of this book to discover whether or no Tom Jones' piece of entomological information was correct; but I shall not enlighten them on the point, for this is a work on legal subjects, and cannot be taken up with recounting investigations concerning the habits of such small things as insects. Saith not the ancient maxim: " *De minimis non curat lex*"?

We had, however, other things to think about ere morning's light again illuminated the eastern sky. Scarcely had we settled ourselves for the night when my wife started up, exclaiming:

"Hear the loud alarum bells! What a tale of terror their turbulency tells! In the startled ear of night how they scream out their affright in a clamorous appealing to the mercy of the fire—in a mad expostulation with the deaf and frantic fire! What a tale their terror tells of despair! How they clang, and clash, and roar!"

"Ha! and well for us that their twanging and their clanging have aroused us; for see! the house opposite is all wrapped in flames, and the wind is driving right toward us!"

Ah! then throughout our house there was hurrying to and fro, and gathering tears, and trem-

blings of distress, and cheeks all pale, which, but
ten minutes past, pressed the soft pillows with their
loveliness; and there were sudden snatchings of
such as by chance lay within reach, and leaving
things which ne'er might be regained; and there
was rushing in hot haste—the men, the chattering
women, and the pattering child, went pouring forward with impetuous speed, and swiftly showed in
the back yard in *robes de nuit.*

I jumped into my pantaloons; fortunately, they
were not like those of Monseigneur d'Artois, nor
was I as particular as his highness; four tall
lackeys had to hold him up in the air every morning, that he might fall into his breeches without
vestige of wrinkle, and from them the same four, in
the same way but with more effort, had to deliver
him at night. We found shelter in the hospitable
mansion of old Mrs. Jones. At the expense of our
friends, we thatched ourselves anew with the
"dead fleeces of sheep, the bark of vegetables, the
entrails of worms, the hides of oxen or seals, the
felt of furred beasts, and walked down stairs moving rag screens, over-heaped with shreds and tat-
ters raked from the charnel-house of nature" to
partake of the morning meal.

At breakfast, Mrs. Lawyer remarked, in anything
but lugubrious tones :

"Well, Mr. Jones, we have got rid of those
rooms without much trouble."

Tom shook his head; so my wife asked:

"Why do you do that?"

"Because I am not quite sure that you are yet

quit of my friend, Mr. Screwhard, your landlord," was the reply.

"What do you mean?" queried my wife.

"Ask your respected husband; he knows more about such matters than I do."

In reply to my wife's questioning glance, I said: "I am afraid it is rather too soon to rejoice over the matter. We must pay rent until we can get rid of our liability by a regular notice to quit."

"But we can't occupy the place."

"That makes no difference."[1]

"Then you had no provision in your lease exempting you in case of fire," remarked Jones.

"Unfortunately, not."

"But why should we pay when we cannot use the place?" asked my wife, growing warm.

"The rule is, my dear, that when the law imposes a duty upon one and he is prevented performing it without any fault on his part, and he has no one to whom he may look for satisfaction, the courts will excuse the non-performance; but when a man voluntarily takes a duty or charge upon himself he must perform his contract, come what may, because he might have provided against all accidents in his agreement."

"And, you stupid! you did not have the lease properly drawn!"

"Exactly so, my female Solomon," I replied, indignantly.

---

[1] Izon v. Gorton, 5 Bing. N. C. 501 ; 7 Scott, 537 ; Parker v. Gibbons, 1 Q. B. 421 ; Fowler v. Payne, 49 Miss. 32.

"Well, I must say," said Mrs. L., "that I fear I am bound for life to

> " 'A wretch so empty, that if e'er there be
> In nature found the least vacuity,
> 'T will be in him.' "

"Another reason is," broke in Jones, anxious to throw oil upon the troubled waters, "that in the case of furnished lodgings, as in the case of a house, the rent is deemed to issue out of the land [1]—none of it out of the furniture [2]—so that the landlord can distrain for the whole rent; [3] and even were he to turn the tenant out, no apportionment could be made for the goods. [4] The law makes no difference between lodgers and other tenants as to the payment of their rents, or turning them out of possession."

"Pray tell me, then, how much notice must we give?" demanded Mrs. Lawyer in tones which would lead one to imagine that she provided all the capital necessary to run the family machine.

Jones replied: "If the hiring of the apartments be from half year to half year, half a year's notice to quit must be given ; if from quarter to quarter, a quarter's notice ; if from month to month, a month's notice ; if from week to week, a week's notice ; and if a lodger leaves without giving such

[1] Newman v. Anderton, 2 Bos. & P. N. R. 224 ; Cadogan v. Kennet, Cowp. 432.
[2] Ibid.
[3] Newman v. Anderton, *supra.*
[4] Ernot v. Cole, Dyer, 212*b*; Cadogan v. Kennet, *supra.* But see Salmon v. Matthews, 8 Mees. & W. 827.

notice he is liable for the rent for a half year, or a quarter, or a month, or a week, as the case may be." [1]

"Still," I said, anxious to contradict somebody, "it has been ruled by a very learned judge that in the case of an ordinary weekly tenancy a week's notice to quit is not implied as part of the contract unless there be usage to that effect, but that such a tenancy will cease at the end of the term without any notice; in fact, he said that he was not aware that it had ever been decided that in the case of an ordinary weekly or monthly tenancy a month's or week's notice to quit must be given. It is to be regarded as a tenancy for a week or a month rather than as a tenancy from week to week, or month to month, determinable by notice. Were it otherwise, such tenancies would, in almost all cases, necessarily continue for a double period, which might be inconvenient to one or both parties. Of course, even in absence of such usage, a weekly tenant who enters on a fresh week may be bound to continue until the expiration of that week, or pay the week's rent. [2] And in New York it has been decided that in a renting by the month, or from month to month, a month's notice to quit is not requisite." [3]

"But surely," urged Jones, "a reasonable notice must be given of the ending of a weekly tenancy. I remember one case in which my father was concerned, Earle, C. J., said that, although it had been

[1] Parry v. Hazell, 1 Esp. 64; Peacock v. Ruffan, 6 Esp. 4; Doe v. Bayley, 6 East, 121; Woodfall, 8 Ed. 176.

[2] Huffell v. Armstead, 7 Car. & P. 56; Peacock v. Ruffan, 6 Esp. 4; Towne v. Campbell, 3 Com. B. 94.

[3] People v. Giolet, 14 Abb. Pr. N. S. 130.

17.

laid down that a weekly or a monthly holding does
not require a week's or a month's notice to deter-
mine it unless there be some special agreement or
custom, he did not find that any person ever held
that the interest of a tenant so holding might be put
an end to without any notice at all. It would be
most unreasonable, he continued, if a landlord were
entitled to turn his weekly tenant out at twelve
o'clock at night on the last day of the week; some
notice must be necessary.   Williams, J., gave it as
his view, that whether it be a tenancy from year to
year, or week to week, in either case there must be
a legal expression of intention that the tenancy
should cease.   The inclination of his opinion was
that where the holding is from week to week a
week's notice should be given, and a month's notice
where the tenancy is from month to month. Judge
Willes, in a half frightened sort of way, as if he had
no doubt he was wrong, considered that because in
a tenancy from year to year half a year's notice only
was required, therefore he could not see how it was
possible that a tenant from week to week should be
entitled to more than half a week's notice.   While
Byles, J., remarked that the notice to a weekly
tenant should be a reasonable one." [1]

" And doubtless he is right. And if it is necessary at all, it must, of course, expire on the
proper day, i. e., at the end of some week of the
tenancy." [2]

" Yes; and a weekly tenancy beginning on Satur-

[1] Jones v. Mills, 10 Com. B. N. S. 788.
[2] Finlayson v. Bayley, 5 Car. & P. 67.

day ends on Saturday.[1]   How would it be, Lawyer, if the landlord rented the rooms to some one else before the expiration of the week?"

"That would amount to a rescission of the bargain, and he could not sue the defaulting tenant for rent for the days the apartments were empty;[2] but lighting or warming the rooms, or putting up 'to let' in the window, will not prevent the owner looking to the man who has left without giving the proper notice."[3]

"I suppose that one cannot leave without notice because he fears that the landlord's things are likely to be seized by the landlord paramount," said Jones.

"Of course you can make an express stipulation to that effect;[4] otherwise you cannot leave."[5]

"Well," said my wife, "I presume that at all events the landlord will have to rebuild if we are to continue paying rent."

"By no means.   The rule is, that a landlord, after an injury by fire, is under no obligation to rebuild or repair the house for the benefit of the tenant,"[6] was my melancholy reply.

Fortunately, breakfast does not last as long as dinner; so this conversation (which had grown irksome to myself, and has proved probably equally, if not more so, to my readers) was brought to a conclusion before very much more was said on this

---

[1] Huffell v. Armistead, 7 Car. & P. 56.
[2] Walls v. Atcheson, 3 Bing. 462.
[3] Griffith v. Hodges, 2 Car. & P. 419.
[4] Bethett v. Blencome, 3 M. & G. 119.
[5] Ricket v. Tullick, 6 Car. & P. 66.
[6] Doupe v. Genin, 45 N. Y. 119.

subject, and I gladly availed myself of the opportunity of going out on business.

Down town I met my old friend, Dr. Lane, who
told me of the tiff he had just had with his landlord. Some months previously he had hired from
one Johnson certain rooms in a fashionable locality, at a rental of a couple of hundred dollars a
year, with the privilege of putting a brass plate
bearing his name upon the front door. Shortly
afterward Johnson leased the whole premises to
Mr. Dixon for twenty-one years. In course of
time, the health of the neighborhood being excellent, Lane got in arrear; so Dixon removed the
brass plate, and refused to let the Doctor have access
to his rooms — in fact, finding them open one day,
and the lodger out, he fastened the outer door, and
so excluded him altogether. Lane sued for damages, and the jury kindly gave him £10 for the
breaking and entry into his room, expelling him
therefrom and seizing his *etceteras*, and £20 for
the removal of the brass plate. Dixon, rather naturally, was dissatisfied with the verdict of these
twelve men and appealed to the court, who, however, agreed that the jury were perfectly correct in
their view of the matter, and that the Doctor might
keep his £30. The removal of the plate was considered a distinct and substantive trespass.[1]   Of
course the disciple of Galen was overjoyed, and insisted upon my taking a glass of something alcoholic while he told me of the little trip that he
purposed taking at his landlord's expense.

---

[1] Lane *v.* Dixon, 3 M. G. & S. 776.

After parting from the worthy leech my brain was rather puzzled to draw a distinction between his case and one decided some time ago, where one Bloxham, a poulterer and a keeper of a beer-shop, claiming a sum of money to be due to him by a lodger—one Hartley by name—locked up his goods in the room in which Hartley had put them, pocketed the key, and refused the boarder access to them till his bill was paid—yet it was decided that what was done was not such a taking of goods as would sustain the action for trespass brought by poor Hartley.[1]   At last it dawned upon me that in the case I was conning over there had been no actual taking—the landlord never actually touched the goods at all — he merely locked the door and kept the key, and therein it differed from Lane's suit.[2]

In another case, a landlord, before his tenant's time was up, and contrary to his wishes, entered his (the tenant's) room and removed therefrom books, maps, and papers, placing them where they were damaged by the rain.   The boarder, not liking such treatment, sued his landlord, and the court decided that the latter was a trespasser and liable for all damages sustained, whether they resulted from his direct and immediate acts, or remotely from the act of God.[3]

Before returning home I called on a friend who also dwelt in furnished apartments.   Far from seraphic was the state of mind in which I found him.

[1] Hartley v. Bloxham, 3 Q. B. 701.
[2] Lane v. Dixon, *supra*, per Cresswell, J.
[3] Nowlan v. Nevor, 2 Sweeny, (N. Y.) 67.

"What can be done to stop that horrid noise? It will drive me mad!" was his petulant salutation.

I listened, and heard the dull, rumbling noise of some wheeled machine being rolled, now fast, now slow, then up, then down, in the room above.

"What is it?" I asked.

"Oh, I know what it is only too well. A foolish young couple live up stairs, and their first baby is teething or something of the sort, and whines and howls incessantly, so the mother by day and the father by night continually trundle it up and down the room in a parlor baby-carriage, making such a noise that I can neither read nor sleep. It is a regular nuisance, and I'll have it stopped."

"I suppose that they don't do it merely to disturb and annoy you, but rather for the good of the juvenile," I remarked.

"As for that matter I presume their intentions are honorable, but that does not make any difference."

"Yes it does; the very point has been decided by Judge Van Hoesen, of New York. To him a Mr. Pool applied for an injunction to prevent one of his fellow-lodgers wheeling a sick child about the room."

"Well, what was the result?"

"Why, as it did not appear that the noise was made unnecessarily, but only from the attempt to soothe the infant, the court refused to interfere with the amusement of the child, saying that the occupants of buildings where there are other tenants cannot restrain the others from any use they may choose to make of their own apartments, consistent with good neighborhood and with a reasonable regard for the comfort of others."

" Humph! "

" The judge added that if the rocking of a cradle, the wheeling of a carriage, the whirling of a sewing machine, or the discord of ill-played music, disturb the inmates of an apartment-house, no relief by injunction can be obtained, unless the proof be clear that the noise is unreasonable, and made without due regard to the rights and comforts of other occupants.[1] And in England it was held that the noise of a piano from a neighbor's house, or the noise of neighbor's children in their nursery, are noises we must expect, and must, to a considerable extent, put up with." [2]

" At all events, no judge can compel me to stay in the house and be annoyed in this way. I'll give notice to quit at once."

*   *   *   *   *

Here endeth the account of our experiences in the matter of furnished apartments, boarding-houses, and hotels. After this Mrs. Lawyer and myself settled down quietly to housekeeping. Our experiences in that line have nothing to do with the subject of this book.

[1] Pool v. Higinson, 18 Alb. L. J. 82.
[2] Mellish, L. J. L. R. 8 Ch. 471.

INDEX.

18.